MW00658258

Spirit of Penance, Path to God

Also available
from Sophia Institute Press®
by Dom Hubert van Zeller:

Holiness:
A Guide for Beginners

Holiness for Housewives
(and Other Working Women)

How to Find God . . . and Discover
Your True Self in the Process
A Handbook for Christians

Dom Hubert van Zeller

Spirit of Penance, Path to God

How Acts of Penance Will Make Your Life Holier and Your Days Happier

SOPHIA INSTITUTE PRESS®
Manchester, New Hampshire

Spirit of Penance, Path to God: How Acts of Penance Will Make Your Life Holier and Your Days Happier was originally published in 1958 by Sheed and Ward, New York, under the title *Approach to Penance*. This 1998 edition by Sophia Institute Press contains minor editorial revisions throughout the text.

Jacket design by Lorraine Bilodeau

The cover artwork is a detail of *The Meal in the House of Simon*, by Pierre Subleyras (1699-1749), located in the Louvre, Paris, France. © Photo RMN — Herve Lewandowski.

Sophia Institute Press®
Box 5284, Manchester, NH 03108
1-800-888-9344
www.sophiainstitute.com

Library of Congress Cataloging-in-Publication Data

Van Zeller, Hubert, 1905-
[Approach to penance]
Spirit of penance, path to God : how acts of penance will make your life holier and your days happier / Hubert van Zeller.
p. cm.
Originally published: Approach to penance. New York : Sheed and Ward, 1958.
ISBN 0-918477-87-5 (pbk. : alk. paper)
1. Penance. I. Title.
BX2260.V36 1998
243 — dc21 98-45766 CIP

00 01 02 10 9 8 7 6 5 4 3 2

Contents

1. A spirit of penance is essential to the Christian life 3

2. Penance unites us to Christ and His Cross 17

3. In doing penance, we must unite our will with God's 33

4. We must develop an inner attitude of penance 57

5. Common sense must govern all penance 69

6. Acts of penance should be done in a spirit of joy 77

7. Love of God should motivate penance 87

8. Acts of penance can lead to holiness. 99

9. Penance brings harmony to the soul 107

10. Embracing God's will is the most perfect penance. 115

Biographical Note 127

Editor's Note: The biblical references in the following pages are based on the Douay-Rheims edition of the Old and New Testaments. Where applicable, biblical quotations have been cross-referenced with the differing names and enumeration in the Revised Standard Version, using the following symbol: (RSV –).

Spirit of Penance, Path to God

Chapter One

A spirit of penance is essential to the Christian life

People are discouraged from approaching penance because they see it from the wrong angle. They think at once of what they will have to do in the way of disagreeable hardship. If they thought of it as turning wholly to God, which is to see it from the right angle, they would be more ready to pursue its implications. They would in fact be spurred on to gather their whole selves together from the four corners of their particular earth and face about — away from self and toward God.

The only kind of penitence that is worth anything is conversion. Not only conversion *from* but conversion *to*. The penitence that stops short at remorse is not a true conversion, not a complete turn. For remorse to be effective it must be supernatural; it must go on to trust. To turn your back upon sin is one thing, and is a good start, but it will not help you for long unless you turn your eyes toward grace.

Once the soul is truly contrite about sin, and not merely crushed by the guilt of it, there is already a stretching out toward the love that casts out fear.[1] There will still be the holy fear of offending God's love, but this is not at all the same as the fear that comes of guilt. Where one fear can be the sign of love, the other can be the sign of its absence. Where one leads

[1] 1 John 4:18.

to hope, the other can lead to despair. Thus, hope is of the essence of penitence; hope is not of the essence of remorse. Penitence assumes also the presence of faith — there can be a remorse that has nothing to do with faith. Remorse is a matter of feeling, a matter of emotional response to certain given facts; penitence is a colder thing altogether, a matter of the will. Penitence can make use of remorse, but has no need to stimulate it. Penitence is a virtue in its own right, strong, realistic, and positive.

Because people confuse the two, drawing upon their own experience of remorse, and having no clear idea of the distinctive element about penitence that links it with the love of God, they view the whole question of penance in terms of external practices of expiation. Faced accordingly with penances to be performed, rather than the disposition of penitence to be cultivated, they draw back.

A man may feel drawn to atone for an act of self-indulgence by an act of self-denial. This is good. This is "doing penance." But penance is designed for something more than this. There is a penitential outlook to be acquired, a habit of compunction. Such an attitude of mind may or may not produce acts of physical penance — it will depend upon the attraction of grace and various outward factors, such as obedience, health, state of life. Such an attitude of mind will most certainly deny self.

It is the denying of self that is the substance of penance; the denying of this or that satisfaction may have to come into it — *will* have to come into it the moment the particular appetite involved makes inordinate demands — but this is simply the way in which penance shows itself. Penance will show itself now in one way, and now in another. The approach to penance lies not in the examination of penances, but in the understanding of the thing itself.

On two counts penances can be misleading. They can be cited as an excuse for avoiding penance itself — the penance of going against self-will — and they can give a false impression to those who feel drawn to deny themselves, but to whom the austerities of the penitential seem out of reach.

True penance is the surrender of the whole self to God. To maintain this surrender — enduring constantly the greater as well as the smaller hardships of life — is to prove the quality of the original repentance, conversion, and break with sin. The man who can face the idea of surrendering himself to God may have little understanding of what he is undertaking, but at least he is approaching penance in the right way. The man who asks himself if he can take on the hair shirt and the discipline is approaching penance in the wrong way. By concentrating on the outward manifestation, he is in danger of forgetting about the thing itself.

The end of penance is God, not more penances. Thus the approach to penance has to be by way of love, not by way of steeling the will to toughness. Penance must have its roots in charity, not in austerity. Austerity may accompany its growth, but it will be a by-product rather than an essential fruit. A certain austerity will even be a sign of true penitence, but it will not be an infallible sign, nor the only one. The infallible signs are humility and charity.

A false saint can give a good account of himself in the matter of austerity, but no false saint can keep up humility and charity for long. A false saint can shed tears of remorse, but five minutes of true repentance can turn him — without the shedding of any tears — from a false saint into at least the beginnings of a true servant of God. An ex–false saint, knowing all the pitfalls, is well placed in the pursuit of true perfection. With him, as with every neophyte, the condition of progress is surrender.

Neither perfection nor penance depends upon careful planning. Planning leads to regimentation. Method and discipline will play a part; the danger is to think of them as the whole thing. Perfection and penance alike rely upon the grace of God as revealed from hour to hour, and if God wills different things at different times, the soul must maintain itself in great flexibility.

In bracing itself to meet the will of God, the will of man tends to set itself in a rigid and heroic mold. The intention may be good, but the manner is bad. Instead of trying to harden in a determined course, the soul should try, on the contrary, to become more and more supple. The mind and will should be trained to wait upon the breath of the Spirit — the Spirit breathing where and when and how He will.[2]

"The word of God is not bound."[3] We tend to think it is. We bind ourselves correspondingly. We are so afraid of shuffling out of our obligations toward God, toward perfection, and toward penance, that we tie ourselves up with resolutions and practices. If the parcel is covered all over with a complicated network of rope, the goods inside will perish because they will never have a chance of showing themselves.

[2] John 3:8.

[3] 2 Tim. 2:9.

A spirit of penance is essential

When we have decided that God is calling us to penance, the procedure is much the same as when we have decided that God is calling us to prayer. We give our whole selves to it — to Him — and leave the details to be arranged as the occasion arises. Just as we do not approach the question of prayer by deciding to practice this or that devotion, so we do not approach the question of penance by deciding to renounce this or that appetite. It is natural to see it in this way, both in regard to prayer and to penance — and perhaps it is the particular observance in either case that first attracts us to the general idea — but the only way of approaching prayer and penance with any hope of perseverance is with the open mind, and with the surrender of the whole self.

The man who surrenders himself to God is thereby renouncing a claim upon himself; he means to transfer a personal right; he hands over to God what has been lent to him by God. He tells God that in fact he has no personal rights, and that what independence he has enjoyed up until now he wants to see subjected to the unqualified control of grace. He puts himself where he belongs — in God's hands.

The man who prefers to approach the discipline of purification and sanctification by giving up now one satisfaction and now another may see more clearly what his commitments involve, but he is handing over only pieces of himself and not the whole. Such pieces may be dear to him, and it may cost him much to see them sacrificed. But as he sees them following one another to the place of holocaust, he has at least the satisfaction of noting the extent of his renunciation.

The other man, without a list before him of items sacrificed, is hampered by no such distraction. He gives himself as completely as he can, and that is all there is to it. For him, the problem is not what to give next, or even how to give more, but simply how to go on in the disposition of letting God take. There is no more generous giving than this, no sharper penance.

To the soul habitually open to the demands of God, there is no drawn-out struggle such as the soul experiences when one sacrifice is offered and another is asked for. There may be a drawn-out suffering, but there will not be a drawn-out conflict.

Most of our mistakes in this matter of penance are caused by a tendency on our part to tell God what sacrifices He would like best. We give Him these things, and then are surprised to find that He has been asking for altogether different sacrifices. We have not been listening to what He has said; we are so sure that we know what He ought to want. Then He comes to us, ready to take, and we are no longer in the mood to give.

If we go on always saying: "I give you this, I give you that," we are liable to add the thought: "See what a good person I am." The emphasis tends to shift from the "you" to the "I." "I am doing all this for you" — with the implication that I would not be doing so much for anyone else, and that you should feel greatly complimented by my attention.

Far better than to say: "I give you this, I give you that" is to say: "Take all." Admitting frankly that it is impossible for us to know what this invitation amounts to, at least we can protest our readiness to meet the consequences without complaint. Admitting also that to yield ourselves up to the process of purification that this voluntary oblation supposes is impossible without grace, we can confidently believe that when God takes us at our word, He will supply the strength necessary to support the outcome.

Certainly God takes when we offer ourselves to be taken, but He does not do so before putting something there to be taken. He puts in us the willingness to see ourselves thus despoiled — which means that He puts in us something of His Son's disposition as revealed when He endured the Passion. "I suffer, now not I, but Christ suffers in me. . . . I sacrifice, now not I, but Christ sacrifices in me."[4]

But from this it would be a mistake to imagine that, having made the grand gesture of surrender, we now have nothing else to do but to sit back and enjoy the satisfaction of seeing ourselves as reflections of Christ suffering. It would be still more a mistake to imagine that we could sit back and see Christ doing the suffering instead of us. Suffering is a work, not a display. The Passion is a darkness, not a floodlit presentation or a parade.

There is nothing picturesque about penance. A procession of flagellants may be very moving, but it is no more Christian penance than a historical pageant is true patriotism. Spectacular penitence bears as much relation to true asceticism as flamboyant devotion does to true mysticism.

If there is one thing to be avoided in the approach to penance and the ascetic life generally, it is dramatization. The picture of that spare figure — the bent frame worn out with austerities, the face drawn with years of expiatory suffering — has diverted many a promising man of God from the pure service of God.

It is the same in the case of prayer: the quiet contemplative kneeling in prayer forms an image in the mind that gets

[4] Cf. Gal. 2:20.

between the soul and God. One of the first faculties to be subjected to the discipline of penance is the imagination. So powerful is this faculty, and so subtle its work, that with these beguiling fancies, it can, before the soul knows what is happening, substitute one set of motives for another.

In deciding to undertake a way of penance, a man must know that he is leaving glamour behind him, that his motive must be to please God, that he will be called upon to bear crosses of quite a different shape from those he bargained for, and that the really effective part of it will be not what he does in the way of self-denial, but what God does in the way of reproducing the Passion in the setting of his everyday life.

Thus the introduction to penance is to be severely objective, realistic, and unemotional. The penance that is forever self-questioning defeats its end; it brings all the interest back to what it is trying to deny. True penance is self-forgetting in the further effort to remember only God. True penance is an outgoing, essentially positive activity. "My eyes are ever toward the Lord, for He shall pluck my feet out of the snare."[5]

There are traps enough in this matter of penance, but to spend time looking at the traps instead of at God is to fall into the worst of them. Grace can steer the soul past every false motive except one — the motive of vainglory. Where a man looks for no other purpose in his penance than that of human esteem, he excludes the action of grace.

For the exercise of penance, as for the exercise of every virtue, the soul must be able to rise above the opposing material pressures. There must be independence — the freedom to

[5] Ps. 24:15 (RSV = Ps. 25:15).

choose what is supernatural in the face of the natural attraction. The penance that is rightly understood increases this independence; the penance that is wrongly understood binds the soul still further to the natural.

Penance is designed to promote detachment, and detachment in its turn both purifies and facilitates penance. Penance sharpens the soul's perception of the ways of grace, and where it does not have this effect, it works the other way. Just as nothing so fetters the soul as misconceived penance, nothing so liberates the soul as the penance that recognizes the direction of grace.

The penance that is inspired by grace and turned toward the fulfillment of the promptings of grace is as much a prayer as it is a penance. Whatever is done in this disposition is done as an act of worship. Whether or not it is performed to the actual accompaniment of prayer will depend upon the individual's presence of mind. Often, indeed increasingly, there will be the explicit and prayerful orientation of the act. But even when the intention is left unformulated, the penance, having Him as its source and end, cannot but be praise to God. It is actual, and not only virtual, praise to God.

So it is that once prayer and penance are found to answer the same need and follow the same end, they can be approached along the same lines and be subjected to the same tests. Until prayer and penance are seen as different aspects of the same thing, neither can be approached in the right way, nor can either be satisfactorily verified.

Unless prayer informs penance, and penance expresses prayer, each is incomplete. Just as in the act of respiration there is the dual process of inhalation and exhalation, so in the act of religion there is the dual activity of mystical receiving and ascetical giving. Neither inhalation nor exhalation is the whole of breathing or the whole of life; neither mysticism nor asceticism is the whole of religion or the whole of life. But in order to keep alive physically, you have to breathe in and out; in order to keep alive spiritually, you have to pray and do penance.

"But is penance as necessary as all that?" it may be asked. "Can one *really* not get to Heaven without mortification?" Our Lord Himself gives the answer to this question when He says that "penance and remission of sins should be preached in His name to all nations."[6]

To all nations: nobody is exempt from the obligation of penance. In some form or another, everyone must deny himself and take up his cross and follow Christ. The idea that penance may be all very well for religious who expect that sort of thing when they apply to enter the cloister, but that it is no part of the layperson's duty, must be a comparatively new development. Anyway, the idea is wrong.

If our Lord attacked those cities "wherein were done the most of His miracles for that they had not done penance,"[7] He will have charges to bring against the generation to which we belong. Never before has the summons been more clear, and never before has penance been so neglected.

Penance is not only for the few — whether for the great sinners who need to atone or for the noble souls who by vicarious suffering take upon themselves the work of reparation — but

[6] Luke 24:47.

[7] Matt. 11:20.

for all who have ever sinned and who claim to be taking seriously the words of Christ.

Just as the obligation of prayer rests on all, so the obligation of penance rests on all. As in the case of prayer, so in the case of penance, much depends upon viewing the matter rightly from the outset. There are many different ways of praying — perhaps as many as there are souls and there are many different ways of doing penance.

Where the soul setting out in the way of prayer would do well to forget what he has read about ecstasies and other mystical phenomena, the soul setting out in the way of penance would do well to forget what he has read about the voluntarily inflicted hardships of the saints.

If a man would approach penance, he must do so humbly, on all fours. He must begin from his knees — in prayer. The grace that comes to him in prayer will give him the light to know both what to do and how to do it. If he stands up too soon upon his own feet and tells God how strong he is to suffer, and what particular sufferings he is ready to undertake in proof of it, and how unfortunate it is that all do not feel as well disposed as he, his penance will come to nothing. There is only one approach to penance, and that is the way of complete surrender to the will of God.

Chapter Two

Penance unites us to Christ and His Cross

We have seen in the foregoing chapter that our Lord required penance to be preached in His name to all nations.[8] In the present chapter we see how the clause "in His name" is the principle of Christian penance. The penance that is preached in the name of reform, in the name of austerity, or in the name of past standards or future progress in any other name but Christ's is not penance but propaganda.

As Christ "suffered in the flesh" — this is the principle to which all that we have so far considered must be directed — "be you also armed with the same thought."[9] "We are . . . joint heirs with Christ, yet so if we suffer with him."[10] The argument in St. Paul could not be more clearly stated: "If you live according to the flesh you shall die; but if by the Spirit you mortify the deeds of the flesh, you shall live."[11] Only on condition that we are "made conformable to the image of His Son"[12] will the Father receive us into life. This means participating in the Passion, and submitting ourselves voluntarily to the discipline of suffering.

[8] Luke 24:47.

[9] 1 Pet. 4:1.

[10] Rom. 8:17.

[11] Rom. 8:13.

[12] Rom. 8:29.

Were we left to ourselves in making reparation for even the least of our sins, we would have every reason to do penance. Some might suppose that without Christ's once-for-all reparation, we would have had more need to do penance than with it. But to think thus is to mistake the point of Christian penance. The point is that because Christ has suffered for our sins, we show our love for Him by suffering with Him. The point is that we are *not* left alone to make reparation for our sins. Christ has gone before us, bearing His cross and providing us with adequate atonement. But the adequacy of His atonement does not mean that there is no more for us to do; it does not mean that we can now stand back, nod our heads, and watch.

The Passion is an appeal for cooperation. "I looked for one that would grieve together with me, but there was none."[13] Although few respond, the appeal goes out to the many. Repentance means "putting off, according to former conversation, the old self, who is corrupted according to the desire of error, being renewed in the spirit of your mind, and putting on the new self, who according to God is created in justice and holiness and truth"[14] — who is sharing in the life and passion of Christ.

"We preach Christ crucified,"[15] says St. Paul, and if the followers of Christ seek to crucify themselves without Christ, they are wasting their sufferings. Suffering must not be wasted: it should be gathered up and offered in union with the sufferings of Christ. Few things are so uselessly squandered as the riches

[13] Ps. 68:21 (RSV = Ps. 69:20).

[14] Cf. Eph. 4:22, 23, 24.

[15] 1 Cor. 1:23.

of pain. Leave the Passion out of account, and suffering is not a good but an evil; take the Passion as the foundation and principle of Christian penance, and suffering is of infinite worth.

"Persevere under discipline," says St. Paul again. "God dealeth with you as with His sons. For what son is there, whom the father does not correct? But if you be without chastisement, whereof all are made partakers, then are you illegitimate and not sons."[16] It is almost as if chastisement played the same part in our regard as Baptism. Suffering, accepted in God's name, brings us into the family of God: we share the lot of the eldest son.

In bringing our penance — whether it is the suffering that comes to us in the ordinary unfolding of life, or the mortifications that we feel drawn to impose upon ourselves — to the penance of Christ, we are not only giving a direction to what otherwise is stray and haphazard, but are finding in Him a new level of living. St. Paul's "Mortify therefore your members which are upon the earth"[17] is not merely preventative, but is also productive. The crooked members become straight, and the straightened members can now move as members of Christ.

There is nothing repressive, still less destructive, about being "crucified with Him, that the body of sin may be destroyed";[18] on the contrary, it is a crucifixion that brings life. "So do you also reckon that you are dead to sin, but alive unto God, in Christ Jesus our Lord."[19] When St. Paul says that he

[16] Heb. 12:7-8.

[17] Col. 3:5.

[18] Rom. 6:6.

[19] Rom. 6:11.

chastises his body and brings it into subjection, he gives as a reason: "lest perhaps, when I have preached to others, I myself should become a castaway."[20] But this is not his only reason. He has just been saying that he does all things "for the gospel's sake, that I may be made partaker thereof,"[21] which means that his self-denial is for Christ's sake, so that he may be made a partaker of Christ.

Everywhere St. Paul speaks of the gospel's making him free, of Christ's making him free. Freedom, peace, and penance go together. Conversion to Christ means liberty, not slavery. It is only those who die and live again in Christ who *are* free. Renunciation is liberative and life-giving. When St. Augustine renounced his Manichean heresies,[22] he did not stifle his intellect but emancipated it. Human reason expands when wholly submitted to truth.

So it is also with all the natural powers of man. Cramped or distorted when used in the service of self, the forces of heart and mind not only generate a new energy when converted to the service of God, but operate in the dimension of grace instead of in the dimension of nature.

The man who turns his back on sin to be reformed in Christ has now a principle of activity within him that gives

[20] 1 Cor. 9:27.

[21] 1 Cor. 9:23.

[22] St. Augustine (354-430), Bishop of Hippo. The heresy known as Manicheism, maintains that a cosmic conflict exists between a good realm of light and an evil realm of darkness, and that matter and flesh are in the realm of darkness. Thus, man's body is regarded as evil, and man's duty is to aid the forces of good by practicing extreme asceticism.

supernatural value to his works. He can say with St. Paul: "I live, now not I, but Christ liveth in me."[23] I love, work, pray, do penance, and express charity to others, and it is now not I, but Christ who does these things in me and through me. "With Christ I am nailed to the Cross"[24] — this is the condition that may not be overlooked.

The faculty that is employed for the purpose for which it was created cannot but find peace and fruition. When every faculty is directed toward its proper object, which is God, there must be harmony, order, and communication of good. The reformation that brings this about has nothing to do with the mortification that is death and disintegration, but has everything to do with the mortification that is life and unity.

The spiritual life is not a matter of killing, but of bringing to birth. You may deny the will and the heart, but you must not crush the will and the heart. Penance is giving up one form of activity in order to allow greater play to another form of activity. The will is not primarily an agent of rebellion; the heart is not primarily a source of temptation. Once it is grasped that these powers are created essentially God-centered, the question is not so much how to curb their activity as how to channel it — how to develop and direct their appetite toward God.

If, in the beginning of his conversion, a man's penitence drives him to muffle his will, empty his heart, close his eyes, and seal his lips, this must be no more than a temporary discipline. It denotes reparation, it administers correction, and it gives the man time to gain control. In order to straighten a

[23] Gal. 2:20.

[24] Gal. 2:19.

warped stick, you bend it back the other way; you exaggerate the adjustment. Once the stick is found to be straight, you do not go on bending it.

The faculties of man are never, since the Fall, entirely upright. There are always corrections and restraints to be administered. But once the excesses of misuse have been repaired, there is a more constructive work to be done. Mortification ceases in one role so as to play a more formative part in another. The self-discipline that was measured to the misuse has now to be measured to the use. When mortification is proportionate to the perfection of the faculty to which it is applied, then is it perfectly performing its function.

Accordingly, mortification is a servant in the spiritual life, not a master. It is not an end but a means. It is a means of perfecting the powers, not of dominating them. If penance once assumes the pose of being an end in itself, it can become not only tyrannical in its demands, but worse than useless to the spiritual life. The man who finds that his one idea is to be mortified for the sake of being mortified must break out from the chains that he has forged for himself, and begin all over again with God as his sole desire, and no thought of penance as an ideal in its own right.

For the joy that is set before us, we endure the cross; we do not endure it solely for the sin that is set behind us. As we have yielded our members to serve iniquity, so now we yield them to serve justice.[25] Having allowed our powers to be instruments of reprobation, we train them now to be far more significantly and truly instruments of sanctification.

[25] Rom. 6:19.

It is not as though we had to look about for some inspiring motive that might turn slavery into freedom. We have the incentive in Christ, in the lives of the saints, and in the example of all who have taken the spiritual life seriously since John the Baptist preached penance on the banks of the Jordan. The principle of all Christian penance is response to grace.

The man who loses his life in this world in order to find it again in Christ[26] and in the next world has learned the principle. He is allowing the seed to die so that it may begin to live.[27] Such a man knows that self-indulgence cannot go hand in hand with full discipleship of Christ. Discipleship is the main thing, so self-indulgence is dropped. This is only elementary reasoning; no great wisdom is required to arrive at the conclusion, and few truths could be more obvious. But before the significant decision is made, there is normally great conflict.

There is conflict all along the line, because there is opposition from every sense and from every emotion. If the senses and emotions have been allowed their independence for years, they will not readily come to heel at the command of the converted will. They have substituted their own particular gratifications for conscience over such a wide area that the reformed character will have to go back over a good deal of ground.

Each appetite, whether physical or mental, has gathered strength in proportion as it has lived for itself. It has subtracted from the life of the whole, drawing to itself an energy or potentiality that was meant to be distributed. The balance is consequently disturbed. Thus an unregulated interest in food,

[26] Matt. 10:39; Mark 8:35; Luke 9:24.

[27] Cf. John 12:24-25.

for example, will dry up a man's interest in poetry; inordinate indulgence of the affections, again, will render a man unfit for serious work. If even a too eager desire for knowledge, study, or progress in one's profession can throw out the due proportions, it will easily be appreciated what havoc can be caused by the intemperate satisfaction of the grosser appetites.

The result of all this is that some of the powers are stronger than they are meant to be, and others are weaker. The strong rebel against the conversion of the whole, and the weak are too enfeebled to support the change. A drunkard finds it difficult to turn to God in penitence, not only because of the abiding pull toward drink, but also because of the lack of pull toward anything else. He has exhausted what were meant to be reserves.

The way back to God will be the way back to the even exercise of all the powers. Penitence is not a tumultuous stirring of sorrow such as many imagine it to be; rather it is the circumspect harnessing of all the faculties under the single command of the enlightened will.

Since in Christ there is perfect self-command — no single part of His sacred humanity developing a way of its own, but all the powers acting in absolute harmony — the more nearly the soul reflects the life and mind of Christ, the more true the penance. Every member or power of the soul must be trained in obedience: the lower faculties cooperating in their fidelity to the higher, the higher faculties cooperating in their fidelity to Christ. Identification with Christ is identification with His Cross. Not until the divine authority is established throughout the whole kingdom of the soul is either the Christ-life or the life of penance made sure.

This means that penance and "putting on Christ"[28] are one thing. If I can train myself to "walk in Christ," I am training myself in penance. If the contemplative life is to "walk before the Lord," then the penitential life is no less. In all that I do and all that I give up, I must accustom myself to keep Christ before me as a practical living model. This penitence, which assumes both recollection and submission to God's will, raises my life and whole outlook above temporal things and places me in the element of eternity.

From such a vantage point in God, it should not be difficult to distinguish between the kinds of penance that suggest themselves: those that are likely to be helpful will stand out at once in contrast to those that are either harmful or wasteful. Thus a man may with an easy conscience shed certain external penances that he has practiced for years. In the light of his prayer and his desire to relive the Christ-life in the setting of his own life, he will see that it is not the hardness of the work that God wants, but the love that inspires the work.

If God wants hardness as well as love, He will arrange for the work to be hard. The first concern from our point of view is to make sure of love. Hardness does not cover a multitude of sins; love does.[29] Hardness is not the bond of perfection; love is.[30]

In the last analysis, we cannot guarantee the measure of asceticism that will atone for our sins, or bring us one single step nearer to union with God. Is it not much wiser, then, to strive for something that can be guaranteed? Is it not better to have

[28] Rom. 13:14; Gal. 3:27.

[29] 1 Pet. 4:8.

[30] Col. 3:14.

recourse to Christ, and to learn from Him a lesson of love? Christ atones for us; love draws us nearer to union. The more we come to know of His atonement, the more we shall be able to atone. The closer we draw to union, the more penitential we shall become.

Our security and our pardon do not lie in any merit of ours. If we trusted in our own power to redeem ourselves, we would be of all men the most deluded.[31] We may have no confidence in ourselves alone; there is nothing to our credit that has not been given to us, and we possess nothing that has not been lent.

"God forbid that I should glory, save in the Cross of our Lord Jesus Christ, by whom the world is crucified to me, and I to the world."[32] When I have done all that lies in me to do, I am an unprofitable servant.[33] "Thy wounds are my merits," and in these wounds I place my trust for eternal life. In the meantime I must work upon the idea of the world's being crucified to me and my being crucified to the world.

At this point the following objection might be raised. "It is all very well to talk of glorying in the Cross of Christ, of imitating His penance, and of walking in His footsteps, but what if I do not feel equal to offering myself for that kind of life? The saints were evidently called to the way of the Cross, but I do not feel that I belong to the same vocation as they." There is an element of humility about such an objection, but there is also a certain evasion.

[31] Cf. 1 Cor. 15:19.

[32] Gal. 6:14.

[33] Cf. Matt. 25:30.

Penance unites us to Christ and His Cross

It can never be right to imagine oneself so hopelessly remote from Christ as not to be able to take His lead. The saints, as they are always the first to admit, were immeasurably behind Him in holiness — He being infinite goodness, they being finite — but they made their token offering nevertheless. If Christ is the way,[34] we Christians are *on the way*. We are followers. We are followers, moreover, in cross-bearing. We come behind Him.

It is idle to speak of coming so far behind Christ as not to be subject to the same vocation as those who follow closer to Him in the procession. You cannot speak of distance between yourself and God. Distance in this context means nothing at all. It is closeness that matters. Closeness is intelligible. Identification with Christ's Passion is an idea that the mind can grasp. It is a fact. It is not a fancy at all, but a truth.

We know that no one can come to the Father except through Christ.[35] He is the way. Without Him we can do nothing. We know, too, that the way He has chosen is the way of the Cross. But although Christ is the one way for everybody, the cross is not the same for everybody. There is one Christ who offers many different kinds of crosses. In taking up the one that He offers to us, we are taking up His, but this is not to say that our cross is the same as anyone else's.

What this amounts to is that not every soul called to identification with Christ carrying His Cross is called to move along the same way of penance. The identification is with Christ, not with this or that act of penance.

[34] John 14:6.

[35] Ibid.

Thus, if a man genuinely feels that his way does not lie in voluntary mortification, he need not force himself to practice any save those imposed by the Church, by obedience, and by necessity. He makes an act of humility and looks about for an alternative expression of his service. Another man may feel particularly drawn to corporal penance — he finds it helps him to be recollected, and keeps him on the alert against sin. For him, too, there are to be acts of humility — they are even more necessary here than in the other case — but he need not worry about the rightness of following his attraction. It is as much the kind of service that he is meant to be rendering as it is not the kind of service that is due from the other man.

So it is that where one man's interior life may be disturbed and stifled by corporal penance, another's is stimulated by it. Each man has to find out by trial what is the way for him. The proof of his choice will be in the effects that it produces. The signs or tests will be considered in a later chapter.

To conclude, the principles to bear in mind as regards penance are: first, that Christ's Passion is its inspiration, foundation, and meaning; and second, that God has not limited the salvation of souls to any one way of penance. All ways are good that lead the soul to Christ.

Seen in this light, the most elementary mortification has significance and deserves respect. A man of one penance may not look down on the penance of another. Means of perfection may differ from one another, but as long as they are truly means, they cannot run contrary to one another. Allowance must accordingly be made for other people's interpretation of the duty of penance. To make this allowance is a condition of being able to choose one's own interpretation.

Penance unites us to Christ and His Cross

Salt comes from water, yet when it is put back again into water it disappears. Our penance comes from grace, and when we put it into the source of grace — that is, when we unite it with Christ's Passion — it is no longer visible. In this lies its greatest safety. Thus it is not the penance that appears outwardly as the most heroic that is the most pleasing to God, but the penance that is secret and the most humbling.

Chapter Three

In doing penance, we must unite our will with God's

Since the whole of man, spiritual and corporal, must return from sin to God, the whole of man, spiritual and corporal, must be purified. If mind and body must alike be mortified, an attempt must be made to distribute the penance so as to assist toward sanctification every part of the mind and every sense of the body. Interior mortification must accordingly touch the will, the intellect, the affections, and the emotions; exterior mortification will affect the physical appetites.

We are told so often that the formation of character is brought about by habits deliberately cultivated that the whole idea induces a kind of nausea. But, alas, the mortification of the will means precisely this. The will doing penance is not a matter of going as far as possible against nature, not a matter of suppressing every desire until a state is reached of placid indifference, and not a matter of issuing harsh commands to the flesh. It is a matter of choosing to live according to God, and of choosing also the best ways of doing so.

"Whether we live, we live unto the Lord; or whether we die, we die unto the Lord. Therefore, whether we live or whether we die, we are the Lord's. For to this end Christ died and rose again: that He might be Lord both of the dead and of the living."[36]

[36] Rom. 14:8-9.

The human will, enlightened by grace, directs its ascetic activity toward filial response and union.

"For if you live according to the flesh you shall die; but if by the Spirit you mortify the deeds of the flesh you shall live"[37] — this is the key text of Christian asceticism. But notice it does not end there. The verse that follows reads: "For whosoever are led by the Spirit of God, they are the sons of God. For you have not received the spirit of bondage again in fear; but you have received the spirit of adoption of sons, whereby we cry: Abba (Father)."[38] The will does not train the rest of man's makeup in fear, but in love. The aim is not mastery but surrender. The will must evolve a technique in which there is discipline without ruthlessness, detachment without supine indifference, and resignation without sterility.

In order to live by this wise and strong rule, the soul must condition itself to wise and strong choices, to wise and strong action. This is where the tiresome subject of good habits comes in. A man must choose the less-easy course so often that when the way is open to sin, he goes on choosing in the way that has become second nature to him.

The law of habit is as present in the moral order as the law of gravity is present in the physical order. The will answers the gravitational pull of habit. A bad will can be turned into a good will only by repeated denial of its demands; only by the law of perseverance in the contrary habit.

Deliberately cultivated habit wears down the inhibitions and impulses that are contrary to it: it hollows out in the rock

[37] Rom. 8:13.

[38] Rom. 8:14-15.

of our natures a smooth passage along which either grace on the one hand or temptation on the other can easily move.

It is commonplace to observe that the will that has been subject to a law that is bad cannot be brought without a struggle under a law that is good. No random effort will effect the change, no sudden resolution, no spectacular reform. The prodigal son has to walk home the way he came, over the same ground, step by step in the other direction. The dawn of true wisdom is not enough, and hatred of sin is not enough — there has to be proof positive in the return to God.

To some, the prospect of a weary journey back to balance and peace of conscience may have so discouraging an effect as to delay indefinitely the moment of starting. But not to recognize the necessity of making the journey is worse.

There is this about the human will, that everyone imagines he can bring it into play with iron force the moment he really tries. "Once I have made up my mind, nothing shall stop me." But this is just where we are so very often mistaken. Whatever we were like at one point, we have weakened without knowing it. Possibly we were never very strong, but certainly we are weak now. Without grace we are helpless. Samson thought that he would always be strong, and that his strength would be enough to get him out of any difficulty, until the day when he woke up and found himself as weak as a kitten. Strength came to him again in the end, but not before he had learned that his whole strength lay in God.[39]

Our wills have to be renounced in grace and built up again in grace if we are to serve God in spirit and in truth. The

[39] Judg. 16:19-21, 28-30.

penance of the will is harder than any other penance. It is also the foundation of all the rest.

St. Augustine says that a man is what he wills. This means more than that the desires of a man are the clearest indication of what he is like. It means that the identity of his nature and the sincerity of his will are the same thing — he could not have one without the other. It means also that what he wills in truth he already in a sense possesses. If he wills to obey God's will, he is already obeying it; if he wills to pray, he has begun to pray.

But let there be no humbug about this. To say merely "I want" relates to a future thing; it must be "I will — by God's grace" — and this ensures possession of the present moment. A virtue (or a hope or an ambition) may be far out of reach, but if I set my will upon it, I am closer to it than to the virtue (or hope or ambition) that I may have immediate occasion to realize but which I have no desire to possess. The will is nine-tenths of the possession.

God does not reproach us for lacking the possession provided we are not lacking in the will. It is the will to discover the buried treasure, as proved by the willingness to go on digging for it, that is rewarded. It is the discovery. The man who wills to love God as much as it is possible to love God, by that very act loves God as much as it is possible for him to do so then. If his will is perfect, his love is correspondingly perfect. Because the saints willed much, they loved much. To them that love much, much is forgiven.[40] The will, love, and pardon: penance is closely concerned with these things.

[40] Cf. Luke 7:47.

We must unite our will with God's

When by true interior penance the human will has been reshaped to meet and identify itself with the will of God, then the soul is capable of great love. Indeed, the soul is then capable of the exercise of the other virtues as well; united with the divine will, the activity is as much God's as the soul's. "I am humble, now not I, but Christ expresses His humility through me. I am patient, obedient, faithful, now not I, but He who possesses these excellences in their fullness is using me as a channel of their exercise." The whole thing depends upon willing the will of God. Without the will of God, the will of man is nothing. All that we could ever do by our own strength would lead to nothing if God did not take our wills and unite them to His. Our Lady could not have become the Mother of God had she not yielded her will to His. Nothing of her previous perfection would have counted had not God's will been hers all along, and had not her will been His.

The purpose of mortifying the will lies in nothing other than in yielding it to the will of God. If our wills were only free of the egotism and independence that keep us from seeing the will of God and surrendering to it, there would be nothing we might not do for Him. But our wills are kept apart from His by so much self that, even with the penance such as has been described above, there is seldom full cooperation.

If the human will were what it was meant to be — namely, a reflection of the divine will — then every human activity would be a work of God. Our works are full of self because *we* are full of self. Our works neither sanctify nor spoil us: it is *we* who either sanctify or spoil our works. However holy or unholy the work is, it is so only because we make it so — because our will is at the back of it for good or evil.

The man who is living in Christ sanctifies all he touches. Whether writing a letter or working a miracle, he is willing according to the principle inside himself, which is Christ. Since his will is rooted and founded in Christ, his whole being is Christ-like, and all his acts are informed by Christ. The discipline of the human will is designed to expand and extend the Christ-life so that self is ousted and everything is seen in terms of the will of God.

"If you cleave to God, God will cleave to you," says Eckhart,[41] "and what you formerly sought, now seeks you; what you followed after now follows after you; and what you were obliged to avoid now avoids you; because if you cling to God, you attract what is God-like, while all that is alien and unlike God falls away from you." This is very much Eckhart's doctrine that if a man's will is right, he is right everywhere and with everyone, and that if his will is wrong, he is wrong everywhere and with everyone. Nothing can alter the direction of the man who has God and God only in His desire. "As no multiplicity can disturb God, so nothing disturbs such a man; for he is one in the One in whom all multiplicity is unity — inviolable unity." It is exactly St. Paul's doctrine of all things being pure to the pure of heart,[42] and of the soul finding unity in the simplicity of Christ.

A man whose will has as its object only the will of God may do other things besides explicitly willing what God wills. He may think of other things besides uniting his will with God's. But all the time, his intention is never for an instant to branch

[41] Meister Eckhart (1260-1327), German Dominican mystic.

[42] Titus. 1:15.

off from God's will to follow his own. Whatever he does, thinks, suffers, and enjoys is assumed to be in virtue of the divine will. To this will his own will, purified now of all selfishness, is united in perfect love and trust.

From the penance of the will, we turn to the penance of the mind. St. Augustine would probably agree that a man is — almost as much as what he wills — what he thinks. That is to say, we choose the furniture of our minds, and live with it. Our deliberate thoughts are our own in a way in which no outward possessions are our own. If they come out into the open they give us away; they infallibly show us for what we are.

But a man should be able to train his thought and his outlook, as he should be able to train a horse or as he should be able to train his will. By applying the right kind of discipline to the mind, a man may change his whole character and his whole life.

It is surely everyone's experience to find that mere mood can transform the scene as presented to the eye. Mood is a thing of the mind, and must be disciplined. Under the right kind of discipline the mood of cynicism can be turned into trust. To the jaundiced, all things are yellow, and it is the function of mental mortification to supply the right colors.

As we have seen in connection with the training of the will, the differentiating quality is not in the outward object, but in the inward disposition. To those who love God, all things work together for good.[43] The penance of the mind helps both these processes: by directing itself toward the love of God, it wins the cooperation of all things in the service of good.

[43] Rom. 8:28.

Even more than what I do, then, I am what I think. It is my thought that prompts the acts that I perform. An objectively good act may qualify as a bad one if the thought is bad that gave it birth. The cup of cold water given in Christ's name will be blessed,[44] while the distribution of all one's possessions to the poor, and the deliverance of one's body to be burned is, with no thought of charity in the mind, nothing.[45]

It is not what you do, or where you are, or how much you endure, or why you succeed that matters. What matters is whom you are thinking of at the time, or whom you originally intended to please. Is God uppermost in the mind, or is self?

"I am never really sure," you may reply, "because although in a general sort of way I suppose I want God's glory, I never seem to feel that either my thought or my action can be giving it to Him." In default of more direct tests, an indirect method may yield better results. What answers, for example, would be returned to such questions as: When I have sinned, do I think with compunction or with self-justification? When I have been snubbed, do I think I have deserved it, or am I at the mercy of self-pity, resentment, and desire for revenge? When I have done something worthwhile or kind, do I think of myself more than of the good I have tried to do or the person I have tried to be kind to?

This penance of the mind must not only correct the wrong thought that is there but also supply for the thought that is not there. It must stir the intellect that is empty, lazy, or irresponsible. The mind must be fed, or the faculty of thought will

[44] Cf. Matt. 10:42; Mark 9:40.

[45] 1 Cor. 13:3.

atrophy. The work of feeding the mind with the right kind of ideas and processes is the positive aspect of mental discipline, and of the two, perhaps the more important. Flaccid minds that look for nothing better than light entertainment with which to fill the vacant spaces of thought must be stiffened by penance into looking for something more substantial.

From what has been said, it will be seen that the main burden in the work of self-discipline rests with the will. Once the will's ascendancy has been secured — in other words, once the essential man has united himself in desire to Christ, and allowed his ascendancy to be paramount in his life — the rest follows: the mind, emotions, and senses are under control. It is the will that puts order into the mind's conscious thoughts, into the heart's conscious affections, and into the body's conscious appetites. Whatever, then, escapes the dominion of the will can be only such fleeting movements as would be accounted scarcely culpable.

This being so, the question of mortifying the affections and the senses can be treated both more briefly and more practically. Although emotion and sense loom large on most people's horizons — larger in appearance, perhaps, than resolution and thought — they answer to rule of thumb. You know well enough when either sentiment or sensuality is running away with you, and you know, too, that when they do, you must pull them up short with the discipline of Christian penance.

In the plan of God, man was designed in simplicity and unity — in God's own image. Every human faculty cooperated in producing both human well-being and the unbroken choice of God. But the moment man turned away from God, he lost his simplicity and unity: his faculties went off on their own, each in search of its private — and deceptive — well-being.

Fallen man is accordingly conscious within himself of fugitive stirrings that struggle for expression, but that, on pain of disaster to the whole, may not be given their freedom. Some of these movements are as articulate as they are insistent, while others work so deep below the surface of ordinary conscious life as to be virtually dumb. It is these strong, silent passions of the deep with which the will has the most trouble.

Where an emotion is perceived by the intellect, or where an appetite is felt to be rousing one of the senses to action, the will knows its business. The issue is clear: yes or no. It is in that submerged area where impulses are only dimly perceived that the will is not immediately effective. How can a man mortify what he does not know? Never appearing as their true selves, whether as fear or sex or envy or whatever else, these tendencies can do great harm unless checked by some sort of control from the seat of human reason and will.

What this preamble has been leading up to is not a plea for closer self-examination. The conclusion to be drawn is that only by mortifying the evil tendencies which you *do* know about can you hope to control those which you do not. To fish about in the largely uncharted oceans of the subconscious for monsters of selfishness that may quite well lie dormant forever and that, even if brought to the surface, might prove beyond the handling of mere good intention, would be folly. In purifying the affections that occupy the heart you can see, you are indirectly purifying what belongs to the heart that never appears.

We have noted above how reason must be trained in the service of love; we see now how love must be trained to be reasonable. The discipline of the affections is nothing other than the direction of love according to wisdom, grace, and truth.

Wherever the heart becomes separated from the intellect, there is trouble. Either reason reigns alone and you get theory at the expense of practice, or else emotion is taken to be the sole criterion, and you let loose the storms of passion.

Nature provides man with two hands, two eyes, two ears, two nostrils, and two feet. Man may not say that in the interests of conservation he can do very well with one of each. To overdevelop one member while underdeveloping the other is to misuse both. The man who sets himself to move only on one leg ends up always sitting down. The man who uses one eye more than the other ends up putting his hand over the weaker eye when he wants to look at anything closely.

For the heart to see in true perspective the objects of its desire, the eye of reason must be kept wide open. The soul must learn to know what is to be loved, and how love is to be handled. Unaided instinct is not enough. Reason must come in to show up the object loved as truly lovable, must be the judge of love's measure. Once the heart steers a course not recognized by the head, there is no holding it; the life of the heart and its direction must come from the life that is life itself, expressing its vitality through the mind to all the other powers of the soul.

Nowhere is it more manifest than here that indulgence brings its own particular penalty. To follow the affections at the expense of the intellect is to deny the affections their greatest satisfactions. Only when love is lived according to reason, according therefore to truth and therefore to love itself, can its highest enjoyment be guaranteed.

Thus the mortification of the affections is brought about not by loving less, but by loving more. The soul must acquire a deeper and more comprehensive love of what is true and good and worthy of affection. Detachment is only one side of the story: the soul withdraws farther and farther from the fallen side of God's creation in order to draw nearer and nearer to its redeemed side. Loving created goods for God's sake and in His name, the soul comes to love God Himself and Him alone. Whatever is less than God is seen as lovable only in the degree that it reflects the love that is God.

Love, essential love, is not divided. God, Love itself, is one. But although love dwells in unity, it manifests itself in diversity. Thus, in practice, there is nothing easier than to exploit a part of love to the neglect of the whole of love. Nothing, moreover, so blinds the soul to its duty toward the whole of love as preoccupation with one of its parts. Infatuation — still more, passion — is the enemy of love.

So the penance of the heart means the ordering of charity in the heart; it means establishing the right distribution. If the affections are allowed to be variable, allowed to run after the immediately attractive, and allowed too much liberty in their manner of expression, then charity is disordered. Charity, exposed to such a dissipation of its energy, may even peter out altogether.

Affection, like courage or generosity or any other virtuous emotion, may err by excess or defect. It is the work of self-discipline to keep the affections on an even balance. If self-discipline sees to the blending of gentleness and strength, of idealism and realism, of confidence and toleration, it should be able to secure the due mean between sentimentality and a too rigid reserve.

Other qualities that come under discipline, if they are to qualify in any sort of relation to charity, are sensitiveness, dependence upon others, hospitality, compassion, and zeal for souls. Each of these is a factor for good, provided it submits to the antiseptic of discipline. Without discipline, you get only charity in reverse with all those dreary habits of mind such as jealousy, touchiness, possessiveness, melancholy, suspicion, fussiness, and meanness.

Without discipline in your affections, you can become so wrapped up in your own love as to be indifferent to everyone else's sorrows. So long as your affection is reciprocated, you could watch the whole world fall to bits and not feel a pang. Selfish affection, like selfish sorrow, is terribly isolating and terribly hard.

A man may be cut off from others by poverty or deafness or blindness, but the gulf that an uncontrolled affection puts between a man and society is wider. It is sad to have to admit that love is as effective as hate in separating a man from his fellow men. When this happens it is no longer love but a parody of love: charity cannot be used to divide charity.

Joy, sorrow, fear, anger, and doubt — all these have to be ordered according to God. The training of memory and imagination must, in the same way, be put on a supernatural footing. Every human emotion must be gathered up and handed over to God. Only when each of his emotional powers is related to the corresponding power in the sacred humanity of Christ will a man be truly mortified in affection and spirit. "For you were as sheep going astray; but you are now converted to the shepherd and bishop of your souls." [46] When the shepherd has

[46] 1 Pet. 2:25.

collected together the scattered members of the flock and drawn them into unity, then has the discipline of our conversion been effected.

Leaving for the time being the consideration of interior mortification, we will consider now the mortification of the senses. To live according to the flesh is, as already noted, death. If by the Spirit we mortify the deeds of the flesh, we have hope of life. "He that soweth in the Spirit, of the Spirit shall reap life everlasting."[47] We must be cleansed, then, "by the laver of renovation and regeneration of the Holy Spirit, whom He hath poured forth upon us abundantly, through Jesus Christ our Savior; that, being justified by His grace, we may be heirs according to hope of life everlasting."[48]

In this unremitting struggle between the spirit and the flesh, we feel sometimes that the source of all evil lies in the human body. Experiencing so keenly the truth that the corruptible flesh weighs down the incorruptible spirit, we begin to wonder whether we are not, after all, more animal than anything else — more animal than either rational or spiritual. But the more we develop the life of prayer, thereby drawing nearer to truth by the light of which we come increasingly to live, the more it dawns upon us that the body is good and made for good. We come to see that evil is far more subtle than the body is ever likely to be, and that its source is in its own spirit.

Corporal mortification of some sort is necessary because, although the body is designed to serve the spirit, temptation normally attacks the spirit through the body. Despising corporal

[47] Gal. 6:8.

[48] Titus 3:5-7.

mortification as being elementary and inferior is as good as denying the necessity of vigilance. It is as good as saying that in times of physical temptation we can trust the strength of our own wills.

Without vigilance, which assumes self-discipline, there can be no security against sins of the flesh. Even with every show of vigilance and self-denial, it is difficult enough to resist temptation, but at least the readiness to mortify the body is a good-will offering that ensures the assistance of God's grace. Where God sees the will to oppose sensuality with practical measures in the physical order, He crowns the endeavor by providing effective opposition in the spiritual order. When the soul, while continuing to apply physical sanctions to its physical appetites, has learned to trust more in God's grace than in any self-devised penance, then there is nothing to fear in the rebellions of the flesh.

If the condition of this confidence in the power of grace is unrelaxed watchfulness, a consequence of its justification must be unrelaxed gratitude. Gratitude should be as much a sign of true penance as it is of true prayer. Gratitude is the surest indication of the life of faith. So long as a man trusts in himself, there is nothing to be thankful for. So long as he trusts in God, there is everything to be thankful for.

Conflict is not sin, temptation is not sin, and failure admitted and repented of is not, any longer, sin. Sin is occasioned by the refusal to admit the danger of sin. Sin is committed by the refusal to prolong the conflict. Sin is prolonged by the refusal to admit the failure.

In some the danger of sin is measured by their ignorance of it. Such souls have become so impervious to grace and so used to gratifying their desires that they do not look upon temptation as at all serious. They do not recognize it as temptation. They feel the same natural impulses that are common to saint and sinner alike, and they fail to relate them to the moral law and to God. For them the natural law is evidently enough. But we know that nature is not enough. We know that without the moral law — God's positive law defining and amplifying it — man sinks to the level of the beast. What can culture, education, and good manners do for the natural man if morals and religion are denied him? Indeed, they can only make him unhappier: a sophisticated animal is a sadder being than one who lives naturally in the jungle.

So the eternal duality in man continues — each nature in him indestructible. Try to deliver yourself from the natural, and the body takes its revenge; try to deliver yourself from the spiritual, and you cannot find rest in the natural. What, then, is the solution? The solution is not to attempt the destruction of either but the development of both.

The solution lies in Christ. Since the problem, with its torment, began with Adam's Fall, the solution, with its peace, lies in the second Adam's[49] Resurrection.

Man must be rescued body and soul, or he cannot be rescued at all. Man was fashioned body and soul, fell body and soul, is redeemed body and soul, and will find his full and ultimate happiness body and soul.

Man was never intended to be complete in himself, even before his integrity was lost at the Fall, but was designed to find his completion in the union of his soul with God. For its

[49] That is, Christ (Cf. 1 Cor. 15:45).

share in the Fall, the body pays the penalty by parting with the soul at death. Until the moment of death, the inseparable companions are in conflict, the flesh lusting against the spirit and the spirit lusting against the flesh,[50] and neither of them getting any pleasure in the competition.

But — and this is the point of the whole thing — there is a pleasure surpassing all pleasure in the mystery that finally triumphs over the mystery of Original Sin. Eternal happiness takes the place of temporal sorrow. The soul that has fought, with faith and hope, the lower nature that right through life has been warring against the higher, will find in Christ's risen life the plenitude of joy. The more truly and vividly this risen life of Christ is lived with here on earth by faith, the greater the soul's present happiness and the stronger the control over the lower nature.

In this life, the inner harmony that was forfeited by Original Sin is never fully restored. But what is much more important is that the essential loss is made good: supernatural life is given back to the soul, and union with God is ensured. If the redeemed man takes up this supernatural life, and directs himself toward union with God, he not only has the ability, by the power of grace, to subdue the rebellions of the flesh, but he can also look forward with absolute confidence to the time when body and soul will live in amity together forever. The doctrine of the resurrection is the complement of the doctrine of the Fall.

Learning from the Resurrection, a man should come to reverence the body where before he either hated it as an evil, feared

[50] Gal. 5:17.

it as a danger, or used it as a means of gratification. The doctrine of the Incarnation teaches him the same lessons. We are baptized into the Mystical Body of Christ,[51] we die in Him, and we rise again in Him.

The Christian's approach to the whole business of "body" should set him apart at once from the heathen and the unbeliever. Our Lord, in His life as in His Church, impresses upon the faithful the necessity of looking upon the body as an integral part of man's nature; the Manichee regards the body as inherently bad. Where the heathen or heretical ascetic proposes to himself the thought of death, the Christian ascetic has always before him the thought of life in Christ. Where the one makes it his resolve to refuse the body all that can keep alive its desires, the other makes it his resolve to refuse the body all that weaken its union with God. Asceticism for one means the minimum of sustenance; asceticism for the other means the maximum of love.

But this idea can be misconceived; can be brought to a too facile birth. Although the maximum of love is the aim set before the Christian ascetic, it is no comfortable ideal that is projected — the means toward its realization may often have to be very uncomfortable indeed. Almost certainly the call to total love will mean the minimum of luxury; possibly it may even mean the minimum of comfort; and in some cases it will mean nothing but the bare necessities.

So outwardly, there may be little to show the difference between the two types of ascetics, and whether they are Christian or heathen. The difference will lie in the intention: one

[51] That is, the Church.

kind will treat penance as an excellence in itself, to be perfected at whatever cost to the body; and the other will treat penance as an expression, as a means, and as an attempt to cooperate in a work that is perfected in Christ and by Christ. If penance stops short at self, even at self-sanctification, it has not learned its Christian doctrine.

"Forgetting the things that are behind," says St. Paul, "I press toward the mark, to the prize of the supernatural vocation of God in Jesus Christ."[52] To "forget the things that are behind" may be part of the discipline that God wants me to apply to the memory. To "press toward the mark" will most certainly mean the discipline that He wants me to apply toward the body. Like "running in the race," and "fighting not for a corruptible but an incorruptible crown,"[53] pressing toward the mark denotes, in St. Paul, penance.

The pressure of this "supernatural vocation of God in Jesus Christ" is constant, is ever-developing, and carries always its one-or-the-other implication. Every denial of the body's love of softness is an act of glory to God and goes toward ultimate happiness in Him. Every renunciation made in the effort to secure more time for prayer, every restriction imposed upon extravagance, every attempt made to keep silence, every denial of fastidiousness in food, every reduction of sleep, and every prolongation of manual labor will not only bring in its dividends in the end, but will also strengthen the soul in this present life.

On the debit side, it must equally be recognized that each selfish indulgence in food, drink, sleep, entertainment, smoking,

[52] Phil. 3:13-14.

[53] Cf. 1 Cor. 9:24-25.

reading, and listening spells a weakening of reserves that subsequent penance will have to reinforce. The trouble is that an act of surrender to the flesh does not stop there; it loosens the restraints. The principle is inescapable: wherever the indulgence is enjoyed for the sake of indulgence, there is an increasing likelihood of further indulgence.

So the soul must be trying all the time to spiritualize the body, steering its appetites *away* from the wrong sort of stimulus, and *toward* the right. Surrounded by every provocation to sin, the soul must at the same time bear in mind that everywhere present is also the invitation to virtue and the recognition of divine truth and beauty. People who scoff at custody of the eyes[54] as being fussy should know that the practice is not only looking *from* but looking *at*.

What is "sown a natural body" must not lose sight of the purpose to "rise a spiritual body."[55] Constrained to live in the senses, the Christian must somehow contrive to "walk in the spirit."[56] The power that is given to the soul can come only through faith; through the grace of the Resurrection. By living in the knowledge of Easter Sunday, the soul can take a voluntary part in the sufferings of Good Friday, and endure the drawn-out waiting of Holy Saturday. Not in Good Friday alone does the Christian life consist, but in repeating the sequence until the dawn of the third day. In this act, which is at once faith, hope, and charity, does Christian penance find its proper function.

[54] This refers to the practice of deliberately turning your gaze away from things that are not meant for your sight or that might, by being seen, lead you into sin. — ED.

[55] 1 Cor. 15:44.

[56] Gal. 5:16, 25.

"For unto this are you called: because Christ also suffered for us, leaving you an example that you should follow in His steps . . . that we, being dead to sin, should live to justice."[57] "All we who are baptized in Christ Jesus are baptized in His death. . . . If we have been planted together with Him in the likeness of His death, we shall be also in the likeness of His Resurrection. . . . If we be dead with Christ, we believe that we shall live also together with Christ."[58]

[57] 1 Pet. 2:21, 24.

[58] Rom. 6:3, 5, 8.

Chapter Four

We must develop an inner attitude of penance

In the fifteenth chapter of St. John's Gospel, our Lord speaks about the necessity of mortification for those who dwell in Him and in whom He dwells. "Every branch in me that beareth not fruit, He [my Father] will take away; and every one that beareth fruit, He will purge it, that it may bring forth more fruit."[59] *He* will purge it; but we must be prepared to assist in the process as well. If we are not prepared actively to cooperate, there is nothing to show that we are yielding to the purgation.

In the foregoing chapter, we have seen that penance can be roughly divided into penance of the interior, and penance of the exterior faculties. In the present chapter we will note a further distinction: active and passive penance. Active penance is largely concerned with exterior life, and needs a code of practical guidance; passive penance is wholly a matter of submitting to what God sends, and so it requires almost no practical guidance.

Passive penance is God pruning the fruitful branch so that there may be more fruit and so that the fruit may remain. Active penance is the branch shedding a twig here and a twig there so as to show to God that it is in perfect agreement with His action. The main work is done *on* the branch; there is little enough

[59] John 15:2.

that can be done *by* it. The primary function of the branch is to abide in the vine and be true to the principle of growth.

Were it not that the principle of growth requires the restriction, and even elimination, of lesser growths, the whole of penance could be passive penance. Active penance is necessary only because man's energy is imperfectly ordered. Some of it is not ordered toward true growth at all, but to decay and corruption. Active and passive penance have to be combined, then, both to arrest the tendency toward deformity, and to promote development according to the soul's higher nature.

If the principle of growth had never been interfered with, there would not have been all this trouble about active and passive penance; about exterior and interior penance. Everything would have developed according to its unfallen nature. But man has to take himself as he is. Penance being now necessary to him, he will want a practical scheme with which to go about it.

Still working from the interior to the exterior as we have been doing hitherto, we can see at once that the passive mortification of the mind is going to be more searching, more effective, and more painful to nature than the passive mortification of the body. For example, it will be harder to accept in faith and love the desolations of prayer than the humiliations of sickness.

The more obscure the outlines of the cross, the greater the faith required and, consequently, the purer the penance. There can be no greater penance than that of suffering passively and not feeling that one is suffering properly. Penance is all the more purifying when the suffering is felt to be wasted for want of making it into a penance.

When the will imposes a penance — whether upon itself, upon the intellect, upon the emotions, or upon the body — the penance may be hard to bear, but at least it will carry with it the satisfaction of achievement. It may be inspired by grace, it may be applied as a necessary measure to avoid an occasion of sin, or it may give glory to God. But because it is self-decreed; because it can still say: "I am deliberately subjecting myself to this discipline," it has less value in the sight of God than the penance that is purely passive.

The penance that is so passive that it brings no sense of achievement, but only a sense of helplessness and emptiness, is more likely to resemble the agony in the garden than a more active penance will resemble the Crucifixion. The word *passion* means suffering, not doing.

It is what is done to us, more than what we do, that brings us into the closest relation with Christ's Passion. The trouble about active penance — particularly if it is more exterior than interior — is that between it and God comes the shadow of self. Helped by prayer, the intention of the penance can pass through the shadow in its upward flight — but what if there is not enough prayer? What if the shadow of self turns out to be the substance of self?

So, taken all in all, passive penance is safer than active penance. And passive interior penance is safer than the penance that is passive but exterior. But at the same time, it should be remembered that the first purpose of penance is to do the will of God and to give Him glory: it is not to play for safety.

God's will may well require acts of mortification despite the possibility of these human elements coming in. So long as self-esteem is not at the root of the act, but only one of the unfortunate offshoots, the act can be performed and the vanity repudiated.

Thus it would be a mistake never to practice active penance, whether interior or exterior, for fear of allowing imperfect motives to enter in. Such a fear is worked upon by the spirit of evil, who is all the time suggesting reasons why penance should not be done. If the Devil cannot prevent a man from doing penance by appealing to his laziness and love of luxury, he does his best to prevent him by appealing to a false fear and a misconceived humility.

If it would be wrong to avoid prayer on the grounds that one might enjoy being seen at it, it would be equally wrong to avoid penance on the grounds that one might like getting a reputation for doing it secretly. Low motives can be laughed off — can indeed be mortified. And even if no absolute security can be found against them (which is bound to be the case anyway) it is always better to attempt a good in spite of its risks than to draw back from a risk in spite of its opportunities.

It is to be assumed as axiomatic, then, that the trials that God allows us in the nature of human existence are to be preferred before any that we could devise for ourselves. To these we must try to respond as voluntarily as to those that are voluntarily chosen. *Passive* in this context does not mean inert, uncooperating, or dead: it means, on the contrary, willing, yielding positively, and being very much alive. The penance is "passive" only in the sense that God is suffered to take the initiative.

Among such penances could be numbered the trials that come from one's temperament and training, one's state of life, one's contacts with others, one's age and health, and one's surrounding circumstances generally. Powerless to alter the conditions imposed by Divine Providence, we welcome the signified will of God. In faith we bow to His wisdom, take it for granted that His love is the explanation of the treatment that is being handed out to us, and submit ourselves to whatever else may yet await us.

The more interior the faculty and the more intense its appetite, the greater the penance and the stronger the faith required to meet it. Thus God may try our intellect by allowing us to feel deluded, by involving us in every sort of doubt, or by showing us the weakness of our judgment. He may try our will by allowing our love for Him to seem wasted, or by meeting our desire for a return of affection from others with indifference or ingratitude or misunderstanding. He may try our memory with a knowledge of missed opportunity and a sense of resentful regret. He may try our imagination by letting us feel obsessed by temptations and dreads. He may try the physical side of our natures with sickness, exhaustion, loss of material goods, nerves, sleeplessness, and the inability to find comfort in any outward thing.

Not one among the above catalog of horrors is an active penance — all are trials coming from the permissive will of God and not from personal selection. Such penance is made, however, by the soul; it is a response to grace. A soul habitually on the alert to serve God by prayer and penance is in a state of positive receptivity that makes these "passive" trials generative. The attitude is the same as our Lady's "Be it done unto me according to thy word."[60]

[60] Luke 1:38.

The faculties that are subjected to passive penance are no different from those to which the will actively applies its discipline. The difference lies in the quality of the acts elicited. Faith and self-surrender are tested to the utmost in passive penance. They are tested in active penance too, but here the opposite pull, because seen and allowed for, is less strong.

In the case of active penance, there is more a need for purity of intention, tenacity, humility, and various other qualities that will be examined when it comes to noting the proofs or signs of true penance. When the will decides to mortify the intellect by restricting its argument, silencing its opinion, or humiliating it with a demand for retractations and apologies, there is pain involved, but not darkness. The soul does not have to make the same desperate acts of faith as when handled directly by God — does not have to hope against hope. The soul has simply to obey and humble itself, and try to maintain enough presence of mind to allow the direction of the affliction toward God.

In the same way, when the will commands the memory to cease its activity of filling the mind with useless longings, or when it commands the imagination to reject its daydreams and pictorial creations, or when it tells the emotion of joy not to be so extravagant and the emotion of sorrow not to go on nagging with its self-pity, the soul has simply to follow the course as before — to keep calm and to refer these difficulties to God.

When it comes to the discipline of the senses, there is necessarily a somewhat different avenue of attack. Greater circumspection will be needed because greater personal responsibility is in question. A man is not accountable for being stretched upon a bed of sickness; he *is* accountable for stretching himself upon a bed of planks.

Before he may give himself to practices of corporal penance a man will have to consider the surrounding circumstances. He will need to be sure that he has the blessing of authority on his resolve; he will have to be clear about what he owes to prudence; he must not allow charity to suffer as the result of his proposed asceticism; and he must have good reason to believe that, in choosing the way of external mortification, he is following the impulse of grace and not the promptings of self.

Not surprising, then, that with these conditions to fulfill, few souls feel justified in assuming voluntary austerities. Nor is it surprising that few superiors, presented with requests from their subjects, give their consent to them. How is a superior to judge whether, besides obedience, the other dispositions are present? The superior or confessor, like the penitent himself, will often have to take the risk, and trust to the power of grace to carry the thing through.

Prayer, as always, is the best surety. If mistakes are made, then in the light that comes of prayer the course can be readjusted. From the active exterior penance of fasting, doing without sleep, or whatever it happens to be, the penance now becomes the passive interior penance of accepting failure and humiliation for the love of God.

Penance in any case is to be judged more by what it gains than by what it renounces, and if it is forced by circumstances to drop this or that renunciation, it is being invited by God to advance in the interior virtues. To think of penance as *giving up* and not simply as *giving* is to look too much at the deprivations, and not enough at Him for whom the deprivations are made.

Without making an attempt here to draw up a list of penances, exterior and interior, that a soul may reasonably feel to be inspired by grace, we should note in passing that there is quite a considerable range of possible penances that can do no harm whatever to either charity, prudence, or humility.

A man in no way endangers his health, for example, if he does not talk whenever he gets the chance, and when he keeps custody of the eyes; nor is a woman's health at stake if she does not paint her face. To dress simply and cheaply, to ban useless questions from one's conversation, never to cut short an interview with people who bore one, to single out one's less attractive acquaintances for attention and kindness, to aim at a high standard of thoughtfulness, and to be as exact as possible in such disagreeable things as accounts, correspondence, and punctuality: in these kinds of penances, a soul does not have to worry about neglecting prudence or slighting obedience. There is little likelihood of one's appearing singular in practicing them, and in most instances they promote rather than offend against charity.

Lastly, and to be treated by itself as deserving individual attention, is the penance that ensures a right use of time. It is more an active than a passive penance, but it contains elements that are interior as well as exterior. Looked at rightly, it is more a positive than a negative discipline: it encourages prayer and the things of God more than it discourages waste and the things of the world.

Even on negative grounds, the habit of playing cards, golf, or any game that takes a sizable slice out of the day or night should be strictly mortified, but from the positive point of view, the mind and body must be given something better than the merest margin for the exercise of religion. The man who plays for longer than he works has got his life on a false balance. When such a man goes to prayer, his approach is liable to be as false as the proportions of his life. In prayer he will continue to be superficial, easily deterred, and light-minded. His prayer will be just another game.

The man who does not even play, but who is idle for long periods of time, will again be correspondingly idle when he prays. Having no reserves, he will very soon find that his prayer is empty. Taking its substance from the rest of his life, the prayer of the man who has nothing to do will be a blank, a vacuum. On the use of what is called "spare" time, then, much in the spiritual life depends. More often than not you will find that the people who are disgruntled with religion, and who belittle the need of it on the one hand and exaggerate the demands that it makes, on the other, are those who could well spend more time in works of prayer and charity, but who instead sit about waiting for the next meal or the next post or the next scandal.

Work is a good penance from almost every point of view. It provides an outlet, it can be made into a constructive service of God, it keeps the mind from self-pity and the imagination from sex, it directs a man's interests away from himself, and it affords scope for wider human relations and, therefore, for a deepening of charity.

There is only one serious danger attached to work, and this lies in the tendency to let it become a neurosis. Thus a man may acquire such a taste for work that it will consume not only all other greeds but all other rightful interests. A man will sacrifice to it his health, his social and family obligations, and his religious duties.

But since the same danger may be said to threaten any activity, even the holiest, this is not a danger that should be allowed to weigh against the implied good. Again, it must be insisted that risks inevitably accompany the pursuit of the highest good. It is one thing to gamble, and another to take one's chance. One may not gamble in the spiritual life, but one frequently has to take a chance on a course of action. The greed of overwork may be as harmful as the greed that leads to overeating — indeed, is likely to be more so because it is not so easily recognized as a gluttony, but is respected instead as a virtue — and must therefore be mortified accordingly.

The more laudable the object, the more disguised is the irregularity in the desire for it. If souls have had to be corrected by St. Teresa[61] and others for the inordinate desire that they manifested for Holy Communion, then it shows how careful we should be to keep the balance. To hunger for work, as to hunger for Holy Communion (or for prayer or solitude or penance), is good. But once the hunger takes the place of the object hungered for, the entire scale of values alters. The next three chapters may throw some light on this.

[61] St. Teresa of Avila (1515-1582), Spanish Carmelite nun and mystic.

Chapter Five

Common sense must govern all penance

The amount of penance that any given soul may be required to do will depend upon so many surrounding circumstances that it might be said that there is nothing to measure a man's penance — he has to find out for himself what he is able to do. But although it would be wrong, as well as foolish, to lay down what penances should be performed in this or that state of life, or in this or that way of prayer, it is nevertheless possible to indicate a few very general rules of guidance.

The light that suggests both the adoption of certain penances and the measure to which they are to be pressed comes partly through prayer and partly through the outward setting of life. To follow the interior impulse without reference to exterior circumstances would be as wrong as to be guided by the exterior, regardless of the attraction of grace.

Through regular contact with God in prayer, the soul comes to the practice of penance step by step. From the vague feeling of "perhaps I ought," which is still largely prompted by fear, the attitude develops into "I would like to try," which is the beginning of love. There may be much imperfection in the experiment — that is, it may be more experimental than loving — but at least it represents a willingness to respond to the Gospel appeal for a concrete expression of repentance. The soul has realized that in the absence of the bridegroom the disciples must give themselves to fasting.[62] To some, the call to penance is more peremptory. Not now a question of *liking* to try, but rather one of *having* to try. It is not an attraction so much as a summons: it is — subject to outside controls that will be considered below — imperative.

Such a summons can be observed in the wider sense when a man living in the world feels the necessity of joining a penitential religious order. The attraction is not one of taste but one of strict need. He feels so strongly that to go on living in the world would be to endanger his salvation that he must enter a community that counters the world at every point. Without the element of penance, he feels that his service of God is necessarily incomplete. The call may first declare itself in fear, will then be strengthened by the force of need, and will find its culmination in the desire to love.

In the narrower context, a man may realize that without a particular discipline, he will become prey to a particular habit of sin. The particular discipline is for him a necessary measure. It would be a mistake to call the adoption of such penance compulsory, because the man's will is still free to choose the habit of sin, but it certainly brings in an element of necessity: it involves a moral necessity. We can all too often live under such moral obligations and give them no attention whatever.

The Christian who is living his full Catholic life should recognize not merely the suitability but the necessity of being a stranger and a pilgrim, of refraining from the carnal desires that war against the soul.[63] He will know that the adoption of

[62] Cf. Matt. 9:15; Mark 2:20; Luke 5:35.

[63] 1 Pet. 2:11.

certain measures and the avoidance of certain pleasures are as vital to his health of soul as corresponding renunciations and undertakings are vital to his health of body. Having arrived at this conviction, he will now have to bring the same practical judgment to bear upon the extent to which these penances are to be practiced.

Turning accordingly from the inward conviction to the outward opportunity, we see at once that there are two influences at work that can be relied upon to register with security: obedience and health. There are other influences — such as those of economy, nationality, common custom, and so on — but in the concrete case, it will be found that what is not covered by obedience or health can be decided by ordinary common sense. You do not need spiritual direction to tell you that to ask for bread and water at a banquet will be a mistaken asceticism, or that to make retreats and pilgrimages when you should be earning money to support a family will be an inversion of right order.

You may say that obedience leaves you a wide margin, that it is not always clearly signified, that you cannot be forever running to superiors for permission to practice this or that penance, and that if you do not happen to be a religious, you have only the broadest laws to guide you.

In answer to that, it is suggested that while it may be safe enough to follow your own choice if there is really no obedience involved, it is safer still, and certainly more perfect, to secure the sanction of authority upon any penance you may want to undertake. For a religious, there would unquestionably be an obligation to secure the superior's consent. In the case of the layman, there is always the confessor to be consulted.

If, at the end of all this, there is still a doubt as to how much or how little you may mortify yourself, you can do whichever you like, and refer the matter more earnestly than ever to God in prayer. Then you will find that in the continued exercise, it will become increasingly clear whether or not you should be keeping it up. The specific tests will be noted in the two chapters that follow.

The second qualification to the assuming of penances — namely, that of health — may turn out to be as flexible as that of obedience. "Am I to consult the doctor every time I want to fast or cut down on sleep? Am I to assume that because a controlled use of tobacco (or wine or outdoor exercise) is good for me, I need never again think of giving it up?"

Health and obedience are not quite on the same level in this matter of reference. Where obedience stresses the positive aspect, health is looked to more for its negative guidance. The project is sanctified by obedience, and it is checked by health. Both obedience and health have the authority to veto a proposed undertaking; but where obedience has the power to supernaturalize the penance, health has only the power to justify it naturally.

Obedience, moreover, once signified by authority and grasped by the subject, gives certainty; health does not. Obedience, for example, can tell you to go against health; health cannot tell you to go against obedience. In your desire to practice a penance of your own choice, you may not go over the head of obedience and cite a "higher good." But there are higher goods than health, and there are occasions when you may cite them. Thus you would be not only justified, but placed under necessity in preferring charity to health. It is in the satisfaction of a private whim that a man may not endanger life or health; in the satisfaction of another's need he is morally bound to. "Greater love than this no man hath, than that he lay down his life"[64] for others. Not to lay it down if the need is absolute would be to fail in charity. Not to lay it down if the demand is martyrdom and the escape is apostasy is to fail absolutely in charity and in faith.

To look upon health as having the casting vote in every decision is to reduce religion to the level of the natural, and virtually to rule out the possibility of penance. Health will always claim more and more attention, and will exercise wider and wider powers of veto. To make your decisions according to health is not much better than to make them according to comfort or money. Like comfort and money, health has the tendency to spread across the whole horizon. Like power, it corrupts. Once you allow health to be more than a guide in this matter of penance, you will find yourself submitting to its dictation. It is a good servant but a tyrannical master. Far more satisfactory is to forget health, except when having to remember it for purpose of reference.

Throughout this investigation, we have been considering the measure to be observed in practicing external and active penance. In the practice of interior and passive penance there is no measure to be observed. In the case of passive penance, the pressure is regulated by God Himself; in the case of interior penance that is active, the soul is free to go to any lengths and need have no doubts on the score of obedience, health, state of life, finances, or any other circumstance.

[64] Cf. John 15:13.

Thus a man may mortify his anger and impose upon himself the strictest rule of patience without having to get anyone's permission or worry about the effect on his physical condition. He may do violence to his curiosity, to his tendency to dramatize, and to his habits of procrastination, rash judgment, over-tenderness, susceptibility, and excitability. There is no law against resisting any of these; they may be treated with the greatest firmness.

To those who would point to the uselessness of penance by saying that it will never make people good who are not good already, and that those who are good already do not need it, the above list, which could be stretched indefinitely, should prove the answer. Penance assumes at least the will to be good; it then assists the progress toward perfection. Even those who can be classified as "already good" must be in constant need of practicing penance. The better they are, the more purely will they practice penance. The nearer the soul to God, the greater the desire to appear before Him without stain of sin or imperfection.

Chapter Six

Acts of penance should be done in a spirit of joy

If a man is to practice penance in Christ, he must go about it unobtrusively and in an orderly manner. Ostentation is as much the enemy of penance as are fitfulness and sudden impulse. Indeed, the two go together. The kingdom of Heaven suffers violence, not extravagance and vulgarity. If we are to take the kingdom by storm,[65] it will be by a dynamic of grace and not of gesture.

Eagerness to convert the world can lead an apostle to preach a program instead of a gospel. Repentance is something more than a policy; more than a piece of propaganda. There is a false zeal that seeks to "sell" penance. Penance may not be chosen as though from a catalog. It is something to be taken up in faith and on the impulse of grace: it is not to be looked upon as a newly discovered panacea that can be paid for in the hard currency of physical mortification.

Penitence is a reticent, even a secret, virtue. When ostentation is found in something as serious and sacred as penance, it is not a mere lapse of taste; it is a vice. The only exception to the hiddenness of penance is when it is practiced in common. The penance here is still to be hidden, but hidden *in* and not hidden *from*.

[65] Cf. Matt. 11:12.

There is no reason why collective penance should be confined to religious communities. It might be recommended to groups of tertiaries, religious societies and brotherhoods, guilds, and other branches of Catholic Action. Under suitable direction, the corporate renunciation of various legitimate pleasures could hardly fail to be sanctifying to the individual members, and to bring a certain solidarity to the unit to which they belong. The main care now would be to see that the penance is truly corporate. Not that it need be practiced in common, but that it should be practiced commonly.

An activity can be practiced by many, but practiced competitively. The desire to go one better than the next man runs completely contrary to the principle of Christian penance. Even the apostle who is combative in his propaganda for penance does not do the cause more harm than the disciple who competes. All individualism, every effort to excel, must be ruthlessly mortified.

But whether the penance is done in union with others directly, or on one's own and only indirectly in union with others, the manner of it must be ordered. This is the second qualification mentioned above, and is a condition that must not be overlooked. "When we praise God," says St. Augustine, "we must be ordered in our praise." What is said here of praise can be said equally of penance.

Just as prayer, whether private or corporate, must involve the harmonious operation of different faculties subjected to common rule, so penance follows the same pattern. The resulting peace will be considered later on in this study — here it is a question of the training that leads up to it. The manner of penance, accordingly, must be intelligent, planned, and directed; not haphazard and borne along on the crest of the wave.

"He ordered charity in me." Penance as well as prayer is brought into the order of charity. Since it is the Holy Spirit who orders charity in me, it must be the Holy Spirit who puts order into my prayer and my penance. Only where there is order can prayer be anything more than a culture, and penance anything more than an experiment.

Although the order must be intelligent and planned, it does not on that account have to be scientific. The natural must be given supernatural inspiration and direction, or the prayer is no more than a mental exercise, and the penance no more than toughness.

Since order involves restraint, there must be nothing eccentric in the performance of penance. Without this restraint, penance becomes exhibitionism, advertisement. Without this restraint, there is a new excess that will have to be mortified. Without this restraint, whatever publicity is given to the idea of penance is discredited; penance theatrically preached and practiced lays the ideal open to ridicule.

Penitents whose ideas about penance are disordered and whose training in penance has lacked obedience, will exceed the measure of penance discussed in the foregoing chapter. Lacking the discipline of prayer, and the light that flows from prayer, they will override considerations of charity, state in life, spiritual direction, health, and common custom. Clenching their teeth, they will go to it, come what may, and in the end they will be humiliated to find that they have been unable to keep it up. God rewards only His own work, and where a work has been undertaken without reference to Him — except for

His name that appears on the posters — there is failure. "Unless the Lord build the house, they labor in vain that build it."[66]

Through their clenched teeth, these false penitents may give good reasons for their penitence, but if they are not ordered in their penance, they will neither wash away many sins nor convert many souls. Certainly they will not greatly help themselves to advance in the love of God.

Without order in their penance — the order reflecting the inward order of humility and charity — the saints would never have summoned sinners to repentance. But we know that right down the ages, the saints have echoed the call of John the Baptist, of the Apostles, and of Christ Himself. They were able to do this precisely because they reflected the order of Christ in the soul. United with Him interiorly, they revealed His discipline. They preached His law and His order. They bore about in themselves the marks of His suffering.[67] They drew others to Christ crucified by showing in their lives Christ crucified.

The man of pugnacious penance has neither the humility nor the charity to make a lasting impression. He has not the submission of Christ. For an appeal to meet with a response that will be kept up, there must be more of cool conviction than burning enthusiasm. Obvious sincerity carries the preacher of penance a long way, but it does not carry him all the way. The only thing that carries him all the way is Christ. On his part, it must be Christ who works in him His unrestricted way, and on the part of his hearers, it must be the belief that he is interpreting Christ to them.

[66] Ps. 126:1 (RSV =Ps. 127:1).

[67] Gal. 6:17.

A man, however deep he thinks his prayer is becoming, and however painful his penance, will never be a channel of grace to others unless he is ready not to appear as a channel of grace to others. It is the grace and not the channel that must be the important thing both to himself and to those whom he is trying to help.

The effect of an apostle's outward charity will be measured by the apostle's inward humility. A soul may be chosen by God to be the channel of His grace to His creatures, but if self blocks the passage, the grace is wasted. That is why, by prayer and penance, the soul must reduce the influence of self until the flow of grace is unimpeded. Mary was the perfect viaduct of grace: free of self, she could transmit the plenitude of good. Perfectly ordered, her soul is the pattern of prayer and penance alike. She is the Mother of Love and the Mother of Sorrows.

As a corollary to hiddenness and order in the manner of doing penance comes joy. The subject of joy will be treated separately as a sign of true penance; here it is considered in relation to the actual performance. There is a distinction between the quality that must emerge as a consequence, and the quality that must accompany as a discipline.

Joy is part of the training. It is a deliberate joy that we are talking about now, not the spontaneous uprush of delight or the settled peace of service. It is the joy that our Lord tells us we must cultivate when we do penance, and that we may even have to assume in order to hide our feelings of melancholy. We must show washed and shining faces when we fast,[68] indicating to the world that penance is not such a terrible

[68] Cf. Matt. 6:16-18.

burden as it is made out to be, and that if only people went in for it more, they would find they need lose nothing of their happiness.

Penance does not, as we have seen, have to be advertised as a universal healer. But it does have to be preached. Preaching penance by word of mouth is not everyone's call, but preaching it by the good humor that is known to accompany it may well be the call of many more than in fact respond to the summons of penance. Looked at from the opposite angle, nothing could be more repellent to those who are setting out on the way of the spirit than to note the sour and sullen aspect of those who have presumably been practicing prayer and penance for years.

"Offer to God," the Curé of Ars[69] used to say to the sisters who worked for him "only what you can offer gladly." This injunction admits of more than one interpretation, but a meaning that cannot be denied to the words is that the penances that are beyond a joyous rendering had better not be attempted at all. If my generosity is not equal to showing gladness in sacrifice — even if the gladness is forced — my generosity is not of the kind that can profitably offer voluntary penance. Better in such a case that I acknowledge the fact, make an act of humility, and look about for expressions of service and love that are within my more limited range.

Although the manner of penance should be joyous, it does not have to be jocular. Heartiness in penance is entirely false; it does nothing but draw attention to self. God loves a cheerful

[69] St. Jean-Baptiste Marie Vianney (1786-1859), patron of parish priests; more familiarly known as the Curé of Ars.

giver,[70] not a hilarious one. If a man is high-spirited by nature, let him curb his boisterousness by humility and mortification — his service of religion should not provide another means of developing it. Penance, since it is founded on humility, should make people more subdued; it should make them glad to go unnoticed.

The spiritual life does not require us to become cringing, obsequious, or diffident. It requires us to become thoughtful for others, as selfless as possible in our decisions and desires, and dependent always upon the grace of God. Penance is designed to teach us this detachment. The manner of it, consequently, is serene; ordered within and without toward charity. There is no harm in making things difficult for ourselves so long as we do not make them difficult for other people; there is no harm in weeping over our sins, provided we weep in secret; and there is no harm even in going to the lengths of our endurance if our penance is ordered in charity and sanctioned by authority.

[70] 2 Cor. 9:7.

Chapter Seven

Love of God should motivate penance

The most satisfactory proof of the authenticity of a soul's penance is to be found in the words addressed by the angel to the women on the morning of the Resurrection: "You seek Jesus of Nazareth, who was crucified."[71] If this is genuinely the soul's intention, the quality of the penance is verified.

If the first guarantee of goodwill is the search for Christ crucified, and the implied readiness to reflect in some degree Christ's Crucifixion, then the second guarantee is faith in Christ risen. The verse in St. Mark that continues the angel's speech tells of Christ's triumph over death: "He is risen; He is not here. . . . tell the disciples and Peter that He goes before you into Galilee. There you shall see Him."[72]

Penance is related as much to the risen Christ as to the fallen Adam. We may think of penance as giving up, but primarily it is an act of receiving. We receive Christ's merits and our share in His Resurrection. In comparison with this, what we give up is negligible. Indeed, without this incorporation in Him, our human penance is literally and absolutely nothing.

Thus, if the value of man's penance depends on the search that he makes for the now victorious Christ crucified, it follows

[71] Mark 16:6.

[72] Ibid., 6-7.

that the less introverted the soul's gaze, the better. By turning inward and ceaselessly examining itself, the soul tends to lose sight of the main objective. The motive may be good enough — a desire to correct the evil tendencies that need digging up and sorting out — but in fact, the process is mistaken. Begun from the other end, God's end, the purification is likely to go far deeper. Again, "My eyes are ever toward the Lord: for He shall pluck my feet out of the snare."[73]

Where penance is self-regarding and retrospective only, it lies open to the charge so often made against it by the world — namely, that it is something morbid and productive of nothing but Dead Sea fruit. Far from being the morbid escape of the introvert, true penance is one of the more virile virtues of the extrovert. It is undoubtedly safer in the latter's hands than in the former's, and for this reason the soul is forever being encouraged to look beyond "this temporary affliction" at the "joys prepared for the just soul in Heaven."[74]

True penance is the healthy expression of the heart in love. The rightly ordered ascetic is no more morbid than the rightly ordered engaged couple, or than children in the nursery. A young man does not say: "I must deny myself the love of evil, the love of pleasure, the love of harmless luxury, indeed the love of everything and everyone in order to have more love to spare for this girl whom I want to marry." He does not measure the extent of his sacrifice against the good of matrimony any more than the child in the nursery measures the enjoyment of his toys against the enjoyment of his mother. Other loves are eclipsed.

[73] Ps. 24:15 (RSV = Ps. 25:15).

[74] Cf. Rom. 8:18.

When the human heart loves according to God, it should grow increasingly objective, outgoing, and unoccupied about balancing rival attractions. If this is the case in human love — everything swallowed up in the man's love for the woman, and the child more interested in the mother than in himself — it should be the case also in divine love. The soul stretches out to God more than it searches in to self. Where there is true love, renunciation is assumed and is taken in its stride.

For the rest, the proofs of penance are found to be the qualities that were examined in their actual operation — what is needed in the manner of practicing penance is now seen to play the part of resulting habit. For the confirmation of penance there must accordingly be evidence of peace, perseverance, joy, humility, and charity.

It is not merely a question of penance's *bringing* peace — a reward, as it were, for outstanding merit — but that the soul finds peace *in* penance. It is true that God crowns the soul with peace, that the soul must strive after peace, and that peace is a gift that is apportioned to the soul's faith and trust; but it is a peace nevertheless that may be found — indeed *must* be found — within the wounds.

This peace, which is essentially in the will, should extend its influence even to the emotions. It would be a mistake to imagine that only in the highest point of the intellect could the soul recognize the existence of unity and certainty. Clung to in faith, the peace that is the proof of penance and at the same time the habit engendered by fidelity should give a certain sense of "rightness" even to the lower faculties of the soul. For something to be possessed in faith, there does not have to be complete abstraction from everything else. The peace that the soul knows in God can be known, without diminishing trust, in the sense of fitness and belonging and being part of the divine plan.

The idea may be taken a step further, and it may be said that, without such a mixture of tranquillity and conviction, the soul is without the surety to which — if prayer is to be practiced without the nagging distraction of despair, and if penance is to be continued in hope — the soul is entitled. There should be *some* sense of having taken the right step and being now in the right way. And this we call peace. To possess such a sense of rightness or belonging leads to an increase of faith. Certainly it does not argue a weakening in it. To imagine that we must go along with no security *at all* is to exaggerate the abstraction. If a person really had no security of any kind, either in the will or the reason or the emotions, it would not be the way of faith but the way of illusion and unfaith.

Peace, then, is the guarantee of other things besides penance. It is the proof of oneness with other members of Christ's Mystical Body, of oneness with the manifold mysteries of the Faith, of submission to the puzzling manifestations of God's Providence, and of a willingness to respond to whatever vocation God sends. While it sets its seal upon the soul's attitude toward these various aspects of religion and life, it is itself subject to the seal of obedience.

Obedience alone, of all the tests, can prove the quality of peace. We may think we are safe in enjoying the holiest peace, but if we are preferring it to obedience, it is not a holy peace at all. Peace is a by-product of the spiritual life, and not an end in itself. To cherish it at the expense of duty is wrong. To use it as a means of altering the decisions of superiors is blackmail.

"Father, if you tell me to do that, I know I shall lose my peace of mind." If the director or superior abides by his decision, lose your peace of mind and gain the merit of obedience.

Just as peace is to be found in penance, so peace is to be found in obedience — not in spite of these things but *in* them. Obedience is the most effective of all penances because it brings the soul into the obedience of Christ, which was unto death.[75] Like charity, obedience is the immediate bond between the soul and Love itself, Truth itself, Goodness itself.

Like charity again, obedience imposes a two-way obligation. The human recipient of obedience must show a corresponding responsibility, as must the human recipient of charity. Thus, in the case of obedience, the one in authority must respect the confidence, the submission, the joy, and the peace of mind of those whom he is in a position to command.

Directors of souls who like to impose fancy mortifications upon those who look to them for guidance would do well to remember that peace and joy are signs of rightly ordered prayer, and that to disturb these qualities without very good reason might be to disturb the whole structure of the soul's spirituality. Directors who answer their penitents' request for permission to fast and to get up early by telling them to eat twice as much as they normally do, and to stay in bed an extra hour may have much to answer for.

The glib excuse that obedience is better than sacrifice[76] is valid enough from the penitent's point of view, but from the director's point of view, there must be careful regard to what is

[75] Phil. 2:8.

[76] 1 Kings 15:22 (RSV = 1 Sam. 15:22).

sacrificed. By all means let the director ask for the sacrifice of his penitent's self-will for the sacrifice of particular devotions and mortifications, but it is a dangerous thing to demand the sacrifice of another's peace of mind. It may be all that the penitent has left.

Allowing that the most perfect sacrifice is that which is made in the name of obedience, a sacrifice must not be used as a weapon against itself. Neither the sacrifice nor the obedience should be quixotic. It is one thing to bow to the will of a director, but another to bow to his whim. A confessor who is either a frivolous crank or a man so eager for authority as to be a serious despot can break the mirror of Christ's image.

But penance has to show other credentials besides that of peace. In the matter of peace, there is a margin, on either side, of possible self-deception. A man can pretend to himself that he is without peace when in fact he has as much of it as any other; and he can also persuade himself that he possesses it when in fact he has only its shadow. So for penance to be verified, there must be the additional evidence of perseverance.

Penance may have to begin with some sweeping renunciations, but unless the pressure is maintained there is no great gain. To start a penance and drop it when the novelty has worn off is the sign more of an unsettled mind than of a good intention. What is the good of a good intention if it cannot support itself in goodness?

A soul of penance must be a soul of patience as well, or the penance will be wasted. We must be patient not only with the particular practice — waiting long enough in its exercise to see whether it is doing any good — but also with ourselves. Patience is part of the penance. To be uncontrolled in the effort to control, undisciplined in the use of discipline, is the mark of weakness.

It requires great effort of self-denial to abide by a way of penance that was assumed in all seriousness and as the result of prayer. Once we have decided what it is that God wants of us, we should be steadfast in that course until a new manifestation of His will presents itself.

If we do not have the light to decide what course to adopt, we should wait upon circumstances as they appear from day to day. We are not expected to follow all penitential courses at once — it would be impossible anyway — but we are expected to be ready always to follow any course that God may indicate.

This is shown by the fact that we are not expected to imitate Christ in every respect — it would be impossible anyway — but as Christians we are expected to imitate Him in some respects always. We cannot do the works of Christ, repeat the details of His Passion, or fast as He did for forty days. What we can do is reproduce His charity in the setting of our own lives, and study to represent in our degree His submission, patience, silence under insult, forgiveness, and obedience.

It must be possible for us, and the appropriate penance for us, to do at our level what Christ did, or He would not have given us His example. Merely because we cannot preach and heal and pray as He did, does that mean that we cannot yield as He did to the Father's will, show understanding as He did, resist evil, follow after perfect purity, or make use of opportunities for good?

The Christ-life, understood in this relation to our own lives, is something more than a thought to be called to mind when an occasion calls for generosity. It is a doctrine that may have to be learned by frequent practical application, but it is a doctrine that must be experienced from within if it is to be lastingly effective and a constant source of further grace. The knowledge of it must grow to be habitual, and the application of it must come as second nature.

Thought of in this way, the Christ-life is more closely related to prayer than to penance. The soul brings decisions to be made, standards to be framed, and situations to be assessed, *in prayer* to Christ's spirit. "What would He do? How would He judge? Where is His lead?" But although it is in prayer that the soul may ask these questions, it is with the combined force of prayer and penance that the resulting light is followed up. The nearer the soul comes to Christ, the closer the interaction of prayer and penance.

If prayer is to be constant, then, so also is penance. Perseverance is a necessary condition and an essential proof. "Walk before me, and be perfect," said the Lord to Abraham.[77] To walk implies steadfastness, a settled way. The Lord did not bid Abraham run before Him until he was exhausted. He did not tell him to mount a camel and ride until he was given the signal to dismount. The words were as much as to say "breathe before me" or "live before me"; it was an injunction to go on and on.

Other proofs of the quality of penance are humility and charity. To the person immediately concerned, these virtues are less helpful as indications than they are to the superior or spiritual director. People do not as a rule see their humility. If they see what appears to them to be humility, they may well be seeing something else.

[77] Gen. 17:1.

Love of God should motivate penance

A man who bends down to measure the length of his own shadow is left with unsatisfactory figures. Humility is not so much a virtue that we see as one that we see *by*. We see it in others, and if those others are practicing penance, we can judge that their penance is genuine and of God.

Even more surely than humility is a sign of true penance, pride is a sign of false penance. There is no mistaking the shadow cast by pride. This disqualifying vice may not show itself in anything so obvious as ostentation or arrogance, but it will betray itself in the end. It will cling obstinately to its particular penance, will use it as a cloak to self-will, will turn itself inside out and pretend to be abject humility. Pride in penance cannot evade detection. When detected, its humiliation will be penance indeed.

Charity, again, is a virtue that acts better as an indication for the guidance of another's judgment than for the guidance of one's own. I can *feel* myself into a charity that is not charity; I can perform some of its outward acts; I can live for a time in a charity of the imagination — surrounding myself with pictures in which I figure with a kindly smile and quiet understanding eyes — but none of this is any use. This is a sentimental proof of penance and not a supernatural one.

Perhaps only another person — and one of spiritual discernment at that — can see whether my charity is proof of my penance or not. The superficial is more easily recognized from outside myself than from within. Certainly I would be rash to go ahead with penance in the sure belief that my charity was above question.

"Is this such a fast as I have chosen, for a man to afflict his soul for a day? . . . Wilt thou call this a fast and a day acceptable to the Lord? Is not this rather the fast that I have chosen: to loose the bands of wickedness, to undo the bundles that oppress, let them that are broken go free, and break asunder every burden? Deal thy bread to the hungry, and bring the needy and the harborless into thy house . . . and despise not thy own flesh."[78]

Isaiah gives us the test of true penance, and, in the same breath, the test of true charity. The motions of penance and the feelings of charity can be cheaply bought; but penance and charity are costly. It must be remembered moreover that the greater of the two is charity. Although they test one another and support one another, it is important that they should be seen in proportion to one another.

[78] Isa. 58:5-7.

Chapter Eight

Acts of penance can lead to holiness

In accounting here for one or two of penance's effects, we are thinking more of secondary than of primary effects. Obviously the first consequence of penance performed under the impulse of grace is, on the negative side, remission of punishment incurred by sin, and on the positive side, a closer approximation to the mind of Christ. If penance is working according to its purpose, it purifies while it atones and it atones while it purifies. In becoming masters of ourselves, we stand a better chance of becoming servants of God.

From self-mastery, then, penance looks to the service of God. Unless it does this, the effects that we are about to examine will not be forthcoming. When the activity of penance is properly launched in the power of grace, the soul will begin to show signs of greater detachment, greater understanding of Christ's Passion, greater resignation to the difficulties of life, and greater insight into the ways of the spirit and the problems of other people.

The human nature of the soul, freed by penance from so much that is material, and directed toward purposes that are spiritual, comes increasingly to live at its highest level. It exists among temporal things, but lives among those that are eternal. The soul's real life is detached from this earth, and finds its true element in God.

Finding that the emphasis is shifting more and more from the natural to the supernatural, the soul comes to reverse the earlier modes of apprehension and appreciation. Where before the supernatural was understood only in terms of the natural — earthly symbols providing the only means by which spiritual things were conveyed to the mind — now the natural is understood in terms of the supernatural.

The material veil that hides from the mind all but the vague outline of divine truth is worn thin by penance. Prayer and faith have now, in the light which is less dimmed by material things, a chance to penetrate. Not only are the things of the spirit more clearly seen; the things of matter are at last understood in their true context. They are seen to be reflections of the things of the spirit.

Although it is prayer rather than penance that brings the soul to this vision, it is penance that clears the way for it. Giving to the soul detachment from comfort, from material ambition, and from the hundred and one distractions that affection for creatures must involve, penance allows the intellect to bear directly upon human affairs. The intellect is enabled to operate in the way that God meant it to, and the affairs are revealed in the identity that God intended to be theirs.

Along the whole horizon of the spiritual life, as along the whole horizon of the natural life, familiar truths assume a new meaning. The soul sees the sufferings of Christ as vital, personal, and essential to the whole concept of religion and prayer. If this was so understood in theory before, it is known now experimentally — the Passion is not a series of facts retold and re-accepted; it is an experience relived.

In the same way, the gospel story is considered not only as history and doctrine, but also as contemporary and continuous Revelation. The Word is made living flesh. "Jesus Christ yesterday, today, and the same forever."[79] The teaching contained in the Sermon on the Mount[80] is heard to echo down the centuries. The voice of the Church and the voice of Christ are one. The sufferings of the Church and the sufferings of Christ are the same Passion. The Christ-life unfolding itself in every age is seen to have a unity and a timelessness to which only a notional assent has been given hitherto. The soul, purified in its understanding and strengthened in its will, is now in a position to cooperate.

The Christian who prays no more than he is obliged to, and whose penance is restricted to abstaining from meat on Fridays serves God from a distance. His religion is composed of obligations. What he sees of religion is more the natural than the supernatural. He sees so much of the natural that unless he is uncritical by temperament, he wonders at the presence of weakness and corruption in something that claims to be supernatural. If this man prayed more and did more penance, he would see the matter more as God sees it. It is not only that he would be ready to make greater allowance for the natural; it is rather that he would see deeper into the supernatural. He would see the supernatural so clearly that the natural would not bother him.

Without penance to clarify the vision, creation cannot but be seen out of true. Once penance has come in, and the light

[79] Heb. 13:8.

[80] Matt. 5-7.

of prayer has been brought to shine upon the created order, the soul can appreciate the value of sharing Christ's Passion with others, can welcome opportunities of suffering, and can want to show compassion to the members of Christ's Mystical Body. It is not a cold benevolence that drives the soul to take an interest in other human beings; it is not even a warm human pity such as one human being may naturally feel toward another; it is a supernatural charity longing to find expression, and meeting in another's suffering the suffering of Christ Himself. It is "like calling to like" and finding itself in like: God is charity,[81] and the charity in one is magnetic in its attraction to the charity in another.

In this process of attraction, it is penance that sharpens the sensibilities, so that eventually God is responded to throughout His Revelation — in nature, in the Scriptures, in the million masks of His face, and in the wide field of public affairs — as well as in the intimate area of the soul's personal problems. To the man of prayer and penance, the work of spiritual direction is approached with a directness and sureness of touch such as would be impossible to the man of slender interior resources.

Practiced in resisting the greeds of the body, the man of penance comes to so steady a resistance to the greeds of the mind as to be independent of the motives that ordinarily prejudice the judgment. With the appetites in abeyance, a man's perceptions are direct and his reasoning powers are able to work smoothly. Such a one will give good advice because it will be independent advice — it will have truth as its object. Such a one will not try to please for the sake of pleasing, nor

[81] 1 John 4:8, 16.

will he give the advice which, in the abstract, he feels he ought to give. He will simply say what he believes that God here and now wants him to say. It is important to secure this kind of man for one's spiritual director.

Together with this almost instinctive right judgment, where reasoning is so swift and direct that decisions are arrived at without the delay of retrospective examination, goes an equally clear insight into one's own weakness and insufficiency. In the light of grace, and with the new focus of vision, one's sins stand out in agonizing sharpness. One is forced now into an even greater dependence upon God. If despair is not to result from this sense of unworthiness, humility must come as a necessary consequence.

Such are the more important effects, direct and indirect, of penance backed by prayer and of prayer backed by penance. But in addition to these, there are many lesser benefits that the soul must come to enjoy in the course of the spiritual struggle.

For example, the practice of judicious renunciation will have a stiffening effect upon one's religious resolve. The seriousness of the spiritual life will be emphasized by such acts as fasting or physical mortification; and still more by such penances as silence under correction, refusal to indulge in frivolous recreation, and restriction of holidays and time given to sport.

Another effect will be the raising of the soul's standards and ideals. Conscience, enlightened more immediately by grace, will be found to demand a stricter account of the virtues. What was good enough for purity before is felt now to be inadequate — the implications of this virtue are seen to be very far-reaching indeed. Poverty (if one is a religious) reveals new shades of meaning, and must be responded to with a greater and more interior fidelity.

So it is all along the line; penance brings to the soul a delicacy of perception with regard to the virtues, while at the same time giving to the will a greater desire to practice them. Nothing, however small, that is capable of being turned in a Godward direction is felt to be beneath attention; nothing, however large, is felt to be beyond one's power to attempt. If the attempt were made in one's own name and on one's own strength, nothing — and one knows this without any shadow of doubt — would come of it. Made in the name of God, the attempt, however frustrated in the event, is already to His glory. If one's penance has taught one nothing other than this, its work in the spiritual life has been fully justified.

Chapter Nine

Penance brings harmony to the soul

∞

Following the idea from the previous chapter, we can recall St. Paul's words to the Corinthians: We seek Christ crucified as our redemption, our strength, our wisdom, and our life in God.[82] "God truly in Christ, reconciling the world to Himself."[83] Christ is the cornerstone,[84] the principle of reconciliation, and the unifying influence in all life, but particularly in the life of God's service. In Christ we are one with others, we are one within ourselves, and we are one with God.

It is vital that we should not only be baptized into this unity but that we should also appreciate its significance. Unless we experience our oneness in Christ, we see life always in division. The service of God should be understood in simplicity rather than as a service of parts. The spiritual life should bring unity out of multiplicity, should reduce the rules of perfection to a single formula, and should allow love to emerge in peace from the diversity of its expression.

All their lives men look for a solution to the problem of life. If they are Christians, they look to Christ. But a Christian may think he is looking to Christ for Christ's answer when in

[82] 1 Cor. 1:23, 30.

[83] Cf. 2 Cor. 5:19.

[84] Cf. Matt. 21:42; Mark 12:10.

fact he is looking to Him only for confirmation of the answer that he himself wants to give to the problem.

Christ's answer is found to solve the problem of existence only if the Christian is prepared to accept it in its fullness. The Christian who is not ready to have more than half his problem solved by Christ — because he is afraid that if Christ comes in on His own terms, life will no longer be the pleasant thing it is — receives only an unsatisfactory answer. It is not that Christ refuses to reply or feels insulted or gives the man only an inferior doctrine and rule to go by; it is that the man's mind is not open to receive what Christ has to give.

It is commonplace to observe that a man has only his own light to act upon, and that if he does not see more, it is not his fault if he makes mistakes. But is it not his fault? Could he not have asked a straight question in the first place? Could he not have opened his mind fully to the light of God's answer? This gets us back to the importance of purifying the mind and its perceptions with penance, and of bringing the soul by penance to a fuller understanding of the *whole* life of Christ. Left to ourselves, we follow Christ in part — in the part that reflects our own nature — which means that we see Him in our image and likeness.

Thus you will have the good Christian man who bases his idea of life and religion on Christ's own words about coming to "bring joy and life more abundant."[85] Such a man feels it his duty to live to the full. He preaches the doctrine of conquering evil by good, he laughs away his own inhibitions and those of others, and he is all for going out among men. "No pallid

[85] Cf. John 10:10.

recluse for me," he says, throwing out his chest, "the more you think of others, the less you think of self."

Only to look at these people in action is to know that they do not have hold of the whole truth. They are admirable, but incomplete. A lot of what they say is true — is Christ's gospel — but a lot of it is their own. Measure them against the complete Christ, and you see what qualities are missing.

Or take the Christian of the opposite interpretation. For him again it is Scripture that forms the basis of his life and of his spirituality. He knows that "to save his life he must lose it,"[86] that he must "die daily,"[87] and that he must "bear about in his life the mortification of the Lord Jesus."[88] Every human affection, if possible every human feeling, must be eliminated. No distracting interest may interfere with the soul's progress toward God — no politics, no art, no natural beauty. Only in repression lies the way of safety, and therefore the way of assured perfection.

But once more you feel that this cannot be what Christ would have advised, cannot be the whole truth. You admire the logic of such souls, but you suspect that the argument has skipped some clauses. You admire the tenacity that keeps these people on so rugged a course, and you find yourself falling back upon the explanation that there is room in the scheme of grace for these very special calls.

Where does the solution lie? We know on the one hand that heedless expenditure of charity and the natural virtues

[86] Matt. 16:25; Mark 8:35; Luke 9:24.

[87] 1 Cor. 15:31.

[88] Cf. Gal. 6:17.

deprives the soul of its full life in Christ, and we know on the other hand that God has not endowed us with His gifts simply so that we may give them up. Somehow the two principles must be reconciled. The unifying element must be found that will bring life into death, and mortification into life. The only factor that will have the effect of preventing stagnation and decay in the doctrine of negation, and that will at the same time curb the display of selfish vitality in the way of too positive affirmation, is the fuller understanding of the full Christ-life.

Once the soul really grasps the significance of what has been received in Baptism, there is no need to deviate and divide. Possessing the life of Christ, the soul's whole concern is to match it in the existing setting. This or that form of life does not have to be explained as a "special vocation": the point of the Christian life is that it is open, under grace, to all.

Every Christian, accordingly, is called to impart charity like an apostle, and to store it up by prayer and penance like a recluse. Every Christian is called to be part Martha and part Mary.[89] Some will have to do the works of Martha in the spirit of Mary, while others will have to combine the contemplative work of Mary with the willingness to serve at Martha's side. It is only the work of grace that can resolve in the soul the apparent paradoxes of the Christian ideal. The seed must die in order to live.[90] A man must divest himself of all things if he is to

[89] Martha and Mary, friends of Christ, represent, respectively, the active and contemplative sides of the Christian life; see Luke 10:38-42.

[90] John 12:24-25.

enjoy all things. A man must be hidden in the tomb with Christ if he is to rise again with Christ.[91]

Always in this life, the Christian will find himself faced with the implication of Christ's submission, of Christ's mortification. The lower freedom has to be sacrificed for the higher one. The Christian renounces a good for something better, new lamps for old. "Mortality is swallowed up by life."[92]

It is not that the lower freedom is scorned, or that created good has to be thought of as evil. "Every creature of God is good."[93] And again: "It is not for thee to call profane what God has made clean."[94] It is simply that the lower freedom must not be misused; the created good must not be sought greedily. Penance steps in to ensure the right order, the right intention, and the right direction.

The mere fact of not having does no more good to a man than having. Some who have little might be better if they had more. Taken in itself, neither the absence nor the presence of goods is virtue. Virtue lies in detachment; vice in greed. It is not even the pleasure or pain, taken in itself, that qualifies. What qualifies is the desire.

No outward thing is to be either condemned or worshiped. It is we who stand condemned by our misuse of outward things — by our worshiping them too much on one hand, or despising them too much on the other. It is penance, again, that keeps the balance.

[91] Cf. Rom. 6:4; Col. 3:3-4.

[92] Cf. 1 Cor. 15:54.

[93] 1 Tim. 4:4.

[94] Cf. Acts 11:9.

It is another anomaly in the spiritual life that penance itself, without the *balance* of penance to correct it, can be worshiped. This happens whenever *acts* of mortification take the place of mortification, whenever penitential practices smother the spirit of compunction and prayer. Thus it can come about that penance, which is designed to liberate, is found in effect to fetter.

Always the soul must maintain the balance of penance; must be sufficiently detached to be able to judge the penances in relation to God, and not only in relation to self. Christ Himself holds the balance, and in Him the soul will find a unity, simplicity, and reality that no outward disposition of duties will secure. The Christian must come to know that, apart from Christ and his life in Christ, there can be no true harmony. Christ is his peace within himself, between himself and others, and with the Father.

Chapter Ten

Embracing God's will is the most perfect penance

In this final chapter, an attempt must be made to bring the practice of penance as outlined into immediate relation with the perfection of penance as exemplified in Christ. Without some sort of ascetical integration, the unity that we have been considering will be impossible. The method accordingly will be: first, to summarize the conclusions arrived at regarding what might be called *applied* penance, and then, to view the whole in the light of what might be called the *infused* penance that comes to the soul in the life-giving spirit of Christ.

"If thy hand or thy foot scandalize thee, cut it off and cast it from thee. It is better for thee to go into life maimed or lame than, having two hands or two feet, to be cast into everlasting fire. And if thy eye scandalize thee, pluck it out and cast it from thee. It is better for thee, having one eye, to enter into life than, having two eyes, to be cast into hellfire."[95] This means that we have first to recognize an occasion of sin when we see one, and not to confuse it with unavoidable temptation; we have then to be ready for renunciation. But there is a third point to be noted in the text: we may not deal out death indiscriminately. We cut off the offending member; we leave the other members to do the extra work.

[95] Matt. 18:8-9.

The implication to be stressed in this text is that we may cut off only as much or as little as is required by God, and only as much or as little as will not harm the essential organism. If we renounce more than a certain amount, we frustrate the purpose of renunciation — we blow out the spark of life that our penance is meant to be kindling.

Man is composed of body and spirit, and by doing too much violence to the one or the other, he may injure the life of both. Man may not live exclusively in the body or exclusively in the spirit. He has to find a way of living peacefully in both. In both he walks through life, wearing a coat without seam.[96] He is not one man externally and another internally; he is an identity, a whole person.

Thus, for a man to forego an activity or a gratification that leaves a gap in his identity is to abuse the virtue of penance. A man may fast so much that he destroys not only the body but also the spirit. When his fasts leave him too weak to pray, he should know that it is time to make alterations in his system of penance. A man may pray so much that he leaves no time or energy for the practice of charity. For such a man this should be a sign to reduce his time for prayer.

Penance must be normal first, before it can presume to be abnormal. We must return to the natural perfection of our first parents in the Garden of Eden before we return to the somewhat unnatural perfection of those who did penance in the desert.

For various reasons it is the most ordinary penance that gives the greatest glory to God and most surely advances the

[96] Cf. John 19:23.

soul in perfection. By *ordinary* is meant actual, chosen by God. The ordinary penance of living in a state of constant surrender to the divine will may well be accompanied, as we have seen throughout this study, by works of active voluntary penance, but always it must be borne in mind that no penance can substitute for abandonment into God's hands. The penance involved in dependence upon the Providence of God expresses faith, hope, and charity. You cannot ask more of a penance than that.

In accepting whatever happens, whether pleasurable, painful, or indifferent, the soul is in no danger of getting caught up in the niceties of active penance. Details that have to do with food, clothing, sleep, and the endurance of other voluntary hardships can distract the soul from the main purpose; they can provide material for self-congratulation, exhibitionism, and uncharitable comparison. Constantly to accommodate oneself, always to remain flexible and uncomplaining, never to assert what one conceives to be one's rights, and patiently to wait upon God's will: penance finds its highest expression in such an attitude. Only when a man can assure himself that he is able to face with equanimity the work, the people, the climate, the food, the leisure, the recognition, and the devotion — in fact, every mortal contingency — that God sends, *and recognize it as sent by God,* can he begin to talk about penance. Penance begins and ends with this attitude of mind. Whatever penances there are in between are thrown in for good measure, are tokens of generosity.

The man who can accept criticism is not going to be spoiled by praise: he takes either with equal calmness. Outward things touch him hardly at all; his one idea is to look below the surface of things and bow to the will of God. For this reason, outward penances appear less valuable to him than inward. He is suspicious of the outward show of penance, and although he may see little of his inward penance, he knows that his whole duty is fulfilled in submission to the hidden work of grace made manifest to him by the signified will of God.

If "blessed are they that have not seen but have believed"[97] is a key text in the life of prayer, it is a key text also in the life of penance. The purer the prayer, the greater the need for faith; so also the purer the penance, the greater the need for faith.

For some, the most purifying of all penances is to be deprived of the chance of doing penance. Such a deprivation is a test of the soul's submission to God's will. In one sweep it dismisses the picture of penance and substitutes the principle and the reality.

So prone are we to stand apart from ourselves and admire the heroic attitudes we have adopted on the horizon of our imagination, that to be forced to stay as we are within the frame of our commonplace selves, seeing nothing of our sacrifice, is salutary penance.

So great is the satisfaction of knowing we are doing something for God in the way of sacrifice, that God often demands of us both the satisfaction and the sacrifice. We have nothing now with which to measure our gift to God, or with which to measure our capacity to give. We have to live now in naked faith, trusting only in Him. So long as we trust in what we are bringing to Him, and in what we are eliciting from Him by our

[97] John 20:29.

gift, we are trusting in self. So eager is God that we should trust solely in His support, that every other security has to be exploded, every other confidence denied.

"Friend, whereto art thou come?"[98] Have you come to warm yourself at the blaze of the sacrifice that you have been stoking up with penances? Or to stand ready at Christ's sacrifice in the darkness of faith, willing to bring to it whatever fuel He may want — or none?

From the *actual* aspect of penance, either applied by ourselves or presented to us in the form of God-ordered circumstance, we turn to the *theological* aspect — that is, how it relates to the mind of Christ.

On an earlier page it has been suggested that the soul should come to get the *feel* of how Christ would view a present arrangement of circumstances, how He would have met a similar situation in His own life, and how he would decide and act. The soul is here consulting Christ, and trying to reproduce His kindness, humility, and love. But this is only the beginning of our "putting on Christ";[99] it should lead on to something more immediate.

"The charity of Christ presseth us"[100] — from within. We do not have to refer back to a pattern of behavior, trying to fit two separate outlooks into one. We do not have to square what is in our minds with what is believed to have been in the mind of Christ. We have the mind of Christ now.[101] It is not a question

[98] Matt. 26:50.

[99] Cf. Rom. 13:14; Gal. 3:27.

[100] 2 Cor. 5:14.

[101] 1 Cor. 2:16.

of what Christ *might* have thought, *might* have prayed, or *might* have done; it is a question of how He *is* thinking, acting, and praying here and now in me.

All this is not a trick of the imagination; it is a truth of theology. It is not a pious fancy but an actual fact. His grace operates in the baptized soul so that a man may come with St. Paul to say that the life of Christ is his whole life. We find our identity, and therefore our operation, in Christ. If we respond to the movements of grace, we are, by the fact of the indwelling of Christ, being moved by Him who is our life. Our thoughts are inspired by Christ, our acts are performed in Him, and our charity to others is His charity — is in fact Himself.

"Yes, but what is the connection between Christ's Passion and mine?" you may ask. "Is the whole story of penance to be summed up in the participation just described, or do I have to relate my suffering consciously to Christ's Passion?"

Perhaps the best answer to this, although admittedly it is not the complete answer, is to say that the soul participates by reproduction under grace, but merits by identification. Thus a man cooperates with the suffering of Christ when he recalls, in his own sufferings, the example of Christ and tries to follow it. But whether he recalls the Passion or not while he suffers, it is the merit of Christ's sufferings that gives any value to his own; it is by Christ's stripes that man's wounds are healed. There is no other name by which we may be saved; Christ is our way and our life[102] and our ultimate salvation.

As to whether we have to do anything of ourselves to relate our suffering to Christ's Passion, we cannot help contributing.

[102]John 14:6.

We are in it, and it is in us. Our lives are part of it. Whatever we do is related to it. When we sin, it is the Passion that registers our sin; when we practice virtue, it is the Passion that merits for us the grace of practicing it.

Our life in Christ secures our penance as it secures all else connected with His service. The extent to which we live in Christ is the measure of our penance and our service. The man to whom Christ is all, the man who has made Christ his whole happiness and good, is not constrained by material considerations any more. In Christ he breathes a new air, inhabits a new world, and expresses himself in a new dimension. When at the call of duty or charity such a man is presented with either physical hardship or humiliation or risk to reputation, he hesitates no more than if the decision depended upon money or health. Because it is a project of duty or charity, it must be the will of God. Because it is the will of God, it is performed in Christ. As long as the work is performed in Christ, it is accompanied by the complete conviction that the attendant risks can be left, to work out one way or the other, in the hands of God.

If, as the result of such action in Christ, the soul is presented with nothing but misunderstanding, ridicule, opposition, and even persecution, then further opportunity is provided for the expression of the Christ-life. The Passion is given further occasion for reproduction. The soul is able to appreciate the essential connection between action in Christ and passion in Christ. And into this united activity the soul's experience is assimilated.

The connection is seen not only between action and passion in Christ, but between joy and suffering in Christ; between success and failure in Christ. With the same surrender to the Father's will, the soul meets each category of extremes as Christ meets it. The soul relives Christ's happiness and peace in the Father's will, and Christ's joy in His disciples' affection. The soul that can accept with submission a share in the shame and ingratitude endured by Christ can accept with gratitude a share in the response enjoyed by Christ.

Within the same week, Christ acknowledged the adulation of those who sang "Hosanna to the Son of David,"[103] and the hatred of those who cried "Crucify Him."[104] It is not so much that one counterbalances the other as that both represent the Father's will. Joy and sorrow, peace and distress, reciprocated love and rejected love: these all find their explanation in the Father's will. Whether or not we accept the explanation, the unity is there in Christ. But if we do accept the explanation, the measure of our happiness in Christ will depend upon our unity in Christ.

If there were any doubt either about the value of penance as an act performed by man, or about the incorporation of man's inadequate penance in the completely availing penance of Christ, we would find confirmation of both propositions in the Sacrifice of the Mass.

The union of head and members in Christ's Mystical Body is nowhere more clearly represented than in the immolation of the whole man Christ. Offered, slain, and living again at the Father's side, Christ renews in us at every Mass His own life. We breathe His spirit as our own, we hear and speak His word, and

[103]Matt. 21:9.

[104]Mark 15:13; John 19:15.

we participate both in His infinitely perfect sacrificial prayer and in the good with which the Father rewards it.

He who has atoned for the sins of the world on Calvary includes us in the act with which He atones for the sins of the world at the altar. At Mass we stand with Christ — although it would be more true to say *in* Christ — before the throne of God in praise, thanksgiving, expiation for sin, and in the perfect confidence that God is honoring the united prayer. The debt is being rendered by the Son to the Father, the Father having pledged Himself to accept it.

There is perhaps no study or devotion that gives us a deeper understanding of the essential elements of penance than the Mass. We find in the Ordinary of the Mass a repeated insistence upon man's guilt, his need for mercy, his hope in God's promises, and his final trust in the grace of forgiveness. From the *Kyrie eleison* ("Lord have mercy") to the Gospel reading, the Mass is an almost unbroken hymn of repentance. The invocation "Have mercy on us," which is addressed to the Lamb of God who takes away the sins of the world,[105] is the motif that runs through the whole Liturgy of the Mass.

Not for myself alone do I ask for mercy, but for all. Not for myself alone do I make my insignificant quota of penance, but for all. Neither the prayer nor the penance that I offer to God is anything of itself — either in the sight of God or to the benefit of others or as storing up merit for myself — but by the alchemy of grace and in the mystery of the Mass, I find the fullness of my service in His sacrifice. Yes, all things considered, the best approach to penance is through the Mass.

[105] John 1:29.

Biographical Note

Dom Hubert van Zeller
(1905-1984)

Dom Hubert van Zeller was born in 1905 of English parents in Alexandria, Egypt, where his father was in military service during the time when the country was a British protectorate. Van Zeller was educated privately until the age of nine, when he was sent for the remainder of his schooling to the Benedictine Abbey at Downside, England. Upon completing his education at the age of eighteen, he spent a year working at a Liverpool cotton firm before entering the novitiate at Downside in 1924. Unsettled and distracted by his school duties and desiring a more austere way of life, he struggled with his vocation at Downside for many years, even leaving for a brief period in the 1930s to enter the stricter Carthusian monastery at Parkminster.

After his return to Downside, van Zeller became more involved in giving retreats and in writing on spiritual matters. By the time of his death in 1984, he had written scores of books on prayer and spirituality, which won him a devoted readership throughout the English-speaking world. In addition to being a writer, van Zeller was a prolific and talented sculptor, whose works grace many churches and monasteries in Britain and the United States.

Although a friend of Oxford-educated Catholic writers such as Ronald Knox and Evelyn Waugh, van Zeller once described his own writing about the Faith as an effort to use "the idiom of every day to urge people of every day to embark upon the spirituality of every day." Written with moving depth and simplicity, van Zeller's books should be read by all Christians seeking to pray and serve with greater fidelity in these difficult days.

Sophia Institute Press®

Sophia Institute is a nonprofit institution that seeks to restore man's knowledge of eternal truth, including man's knowledge of his own nature, his relation to other persons, and his relation to God.

Sophia Institute Press® serves this end in numerous ways. It publishes translations of foreign works to make them accessible to English-speaking readers. It brings out-of-print books back into print. And it publishes important new books that fulfill the ideals of Sophia Institute. These books afford readers a rich source of the enduring wisdom of mankind. Sophia Institute Press® makes these high-quality books available to the general public by using advanced technology and by soliciting donations to subsidize its general publishing costs.

Your generosity can help Sophia Institute Press® to provide the public with editions of works containing the enduring wisdom of the ages. Please send your tax-deductible contribution to the address below. Your questions, comments, and suggestions are also welcome.

For your free catalog, call:
Toll-free: 1-800-888-9344

or write:

Sophia Institute Press®
Box 5284, Manchester, NH 03108

www.sophiainstitute.com